WALKING
THE
CIRCLE

PRISON
CHRONICLES

WALKING THE CIRCLE

PRISON CHRONICLES

J Tony Serra

FOREWARD & CUSTOMER ALERT
By
Herbert Gold

GRIZZLY PEAK PRESS

Kensington, California

For information contact:
GRIZZLY PEAK PRESS
350 Berkeley Park Boulevard
Kensington, California 94707
www.grizzlypeakpress.com

Walking the Circle: Prison Chronicles
is published by Daniel N. David
and is distributed by
Grizzly Peak Press

ISBN Number: 978-0-9839264-1-2
Library of Congress Number: 2012938000

Printed in the United States of America

TONY SERRA, DELECTABLE MOUNTAIN
Foreword & Customer Alert By Herbert Gold

A life filled with passion, trouble, and general shit-kicking may be the best life to have, but probably only if you are Tony Serra, wily defense lawyer, generous supporter of perilous causes, devoted custodian of just about everyone except himself. Recently, he continued his mission of disruptive merry-making while incarcerated for a little matter of federal taxes he decided not to offer a federal government which he considers hostile to the poor, immigrants, Native Americans, and folks who enjoy a bit of inner transportation by means of forbidden substances.

In the matter of Tony Serra vs. the System, the conflict has gone on for more than forty years. We don't yet know who will come out the victor, but we know who should.

If you wish to follow his program, make sure you are Tony Serra in order to do it properly. He is what the anarchist poet e.e. cummings called a "delectable mountain." Although, unlike cummings, Serra has skipped the revolutionary gesture of spelling his name without capital letters, I've admired him over his long career as the used-car-driving, used-clothes-wearing, used-hair-getting attorney who turned his back on riches he could have accumulated in favor of making his life a festival of principled rebellion. It is a festival with at its basis a deep moral mission: Tony Serra must change the world. He doesn't mind performing this task through incremental acts of both suave persuasion and stubborn disobedience.

His book invites us to partake of his compassionate and laughing outrage as he continues assiduous practice of the law while sharing the ungourmet food, turbulent surroundings, and curious bunking arrangements of the U.S. prison network. Of course, if you are one who sleeps contentedly among your own nightmares, you won't have two movies made from versions of your life and career. Well, we can't have everything. But at least we have this engrossing, informative, and ~ say it loud - delightful evocation of the experience.

One of the Tony-inspired films starred James Woods, who reflected the agitator's intensity but not his grace, and the other starred Gene Hackman, who evoked Tony's humor but not the charm which has gained him a passionate following. (If he were a Kennedy, it would more elevatedly be called "charisma.") Readers of these notes are invited to live a few of the paradoxes of a lawyer who got out of federal detention and promptly sued the government on behalf of his fellow prisoners for the scandal of their unfair hourly wages.

This was Tony Serra's third conviction for willful and principled avoidance of taxes. It isn't that he loves prison or the hassles involving his law license. Sometimes he wails with pain, sometimes he coolly judges, sometimes he wittily surveys, sometimes -no, always -his spirit expresses compassion for the woebegone of this world. (Less, of course, for the system-that is, not all for the System which put him and others in Lompoc Federal.) He treated the joint as a Buddhist retreat for him but with the significant modification that he spent less time lifting weights in the yard and more time battling on behalf of his fellow inmates. Also he wrote a book. You'd have to say a modified Buddhist retreat with a non-Buddhist sauce of agitation, literary practice, and social networking alongside men habituated to anti-social networking.

Not only a memoir of a prison adventure, the book can also function as an instructional manual in the procedures of happy survival. For example, the lead attorney in the Tony Serra Law Offices is a forty-year user of marijuana, which he explains makes a more beautiful world for him than alcohol, which seems to be the helper of choice for most criminal defense lawyers. However, marijuana was unauthorized, not properly available during his incarceration. He suffered no withdrawal pangs; good blissy recollections plus flash-backs, kept him in touch with spirit, color and transcendence of the self. So if, dear reader, you too are a forty-year smoker or brownie-muncher, don't worry about your stay behind bars.

There are other more dire adventures to be recounted in the short bursts of chapter energy which follow the pages of this Customer Alert.

Once I lived through a wedding where the ceremony was legally performed by Tony Serra in one of byproduct careers as a Universal Life minister. The groom, a distinguished psychiatrist, wept with joy, and it seemed to those of us who were guests, constituting the supporting cast, jury and goodie-munchers, that his tears expressed not only the distinguished psychiatrist's joy at finding the woman of his dreams but also his response to his legal defense maestro-minister's eloquent ramble through world-historical evocations of human possibility.

In another legal context, the sublime richness of a festive life was celebrated. May, dear reader, have the good luck to be either defended or married by Tony Serra. Or if not you, then at least me.

CONTENTS

This book is dedicated to the ongoing inmate struggle for justice.

THE
PRISON
CHRONICLES

IT'S FOR MY FRIEND, HE SAID

Friday night at Lompoc Federal Prison Camp: after a dinner of battered deep fried chicken strips, canned corn, faded green lettuce and a banana, I walked the circle around the camp alone tonight. The muscles around my two hip implants hurt a little, five days of unaccustomed physical work had stiffened them up. I walked slowly and stiff legged. The fog had come in early, the air was a bit chilled, and my spirits were elevated.

Toward the end of the circle, near the weekend visiting area, an inmate acquaintance - not a friend - greeted me. "I've been looking for you," he said. For me, sometimes solitude is precious. I resented the intrusion but quickly quashed the resentment. He had to see me "privately". It was a matter of importance. I knew he needed legal advice. "I'm suspended," I thought but I concluded "talk" is not "practicing"! I said "sure". We walked to a secluded area, and sat on a fence. We turned toward each other. He was young, tall, athletic looking, with puzzled demeanor.

He told me, "You will never get to know me. I am leaving in two weeks, but I need a favor." I said "sure" again.

I am a lawyer; it's like a doctor. You cannot deny services to the needy.

"It's for my friend," he said. "He's truly innocent." "He has long sentence." "His appeal is over; he lost. He needs a writ of habeas corpus."

I told him I was not an appellate lawyer and that I was suspended for six months, but I know appellate issues because trial lawyers must preserve appellate issues on the record for appeal purposes if the case is lost. I asked what are the issues that his friend appealed upon and lost.

1

He didn't know; all he knew was his friend was factually innocent; that a government material witness had perjured himself at trial against his friend. He was dismayed and puzzled. He strongly believed in his friend's innocence.

I outlined some of the areas where writs are valid: incompetency of his trial counsel; newly discovered exonerating evidence; attorney-client conflict of interest; provable perjury at the trial. The list was short. My acquaintance seemed unable to understand. "But he's innocent." he kept saying.

I told him that many innocent defendants are found guilty; that appeal or writ issues seldom address that situation. I said if it could be shown that someone else committed the crime that would be a viable writ issue. He responded that it was the lying informant who had committed the crime. I told him that was just one man's word against another. I asked, "could you get some corroboration?" He said he didn't know.

I thought the matter was hopeless. I didn't want to tell him that. He wanted so badly to clear his friend. We sat in silence a long time on the fence poles.

I give him some hope, I said get me the appellate pleadings, the Appellant's Opening Brief; the Government's Reply; Appellant's Final Closing Brief. I will read them. Then I'll know the case and the appeal issues. After that we can discuss it again. Maybe something good will emerge.

The muscles in his face loosened. He felt better. He could tell his friend there is some hope. There are hundreds of these scenarios in a prison camp.

THE LAWN WATERER

The sun pours like lava from the sky. A solitary green uniformed man stands apart, alone, watering the vast empty equally green lawn.

White tangled hair falls from under an equally white baseball cap, shielding him from sun. An orange hose in his right hand extends the rays of water to the grass.

This is a prison camp. He is a prisoner. He waters lawns all day in the burning heat. He is in a trance. His thoughts are melting. His eyes brimmed with tears, look through the spray flooding from his hose. He sees visions.

He sees shiny black crows through his waterfall. They are lawyers. They are taking flight from his mind. He sees rainbows in the water spray. They are his children of shining colors.

He sees the droplets from a face. It is the face of his beloved. She smiles love from the liquid prison. Now he talks to her; he talks to the water flowing. He says, "Vicki, I love you."

Just like in a Western saloon fight movie, the swinging doors banged open and Vincent Hallinan, the role model attorney of my career, pushed a large Brooks Brothers-suited, corporate-looking lawyer through the door. Vince had him by the scruff of his tie and put him up against the wall right outside the court and let them have it – a straight right hook to his jaw. The lawyer collapsed on the spot. I said to myself, "Wow! This practice of law is going to be fun!"

A WEED

By the side of a well-traveled walkway to the dining room, or the "chow hall", at the corner of lawns and an asphalt parking area for camp buses and vehicles – a small triangle of cactus and bulbous plants stand brazenly in the sun. The same sprinkler that waters the lawn falls on this island of plants and cactus, thus it prospers not withstanding its location in a traffic zone.

I water that area by turning on and off the lawn sprinkler system, and as a consequence, I watch the plants there rise and fall with the weeks and months passing.

A surprise enticed my imagination. A wondrous weed sprouted. It was singular.: a faded green in color, thick stalked, and as it grew, it showed multiple limbs. The leaves were curly and fuzzy. It thrived on the water and sun. It had no fear of cactus or bulb. Between them it shot up sturdy and straight. Its arms like the arms of a Buddha, reaching upward toward the sky. The arms and the main stalk stood about 3 _ feet high. Leaved fingers with flower buds developed. Some of the buds at the top opened, only in the hottest time of day, showing a torrid yellow petaled flower with an orange center. There were so many buds on the healthy upshot that soon it would be an Xmas tree in a parking lot area in a prison camp. What a boon! What a gift!

Yesterday I happened to walk by a garbage can close by. I saw my glorious plant sticking out of it. Still Green – still alive but fatally wrenched from its spot in the small plot of earth. Its dozens of buds will never open. It will join the trash and garbage at the dump.

Someone had recognized this beautiful mysterious growth as a "weed," and ripped it from its life – it's place of prosperity. So it is for all in a prison. We are all like growing plants, with unopened buds, but like weeds plucked and discarded, never to fully flower.

California Civil Code Section 3523.

For every wrong there is a remedy.

Enacted 1872.

But don't bet on it!

SHAVED HEADS

Many prison appearance styles find a place in outside prison cultures, either of limited or general adaptation. Language idioms, the knuckle-to-knuckle hit rather than handshake, talking while squatting; tattooing gang signs and colors, and most currently shaved "heads and beanie hats."

Shaved heads is a military, athletic, prison "look" that is rapidly spreading inside prison and outside prison. Invariably it started with blacks and skinhead white supremacists but now it is prevalent in prison throughout all races and cultures. Blacks, Hispanics, Asians and non-skinhead whites have shaved heads. Almost half of the prisoners at Lompoc Camp have shaved their heads.

It appears to be a "masculine" statement. Weight lifting, tattoos on arms, legs, bodies, necks and even on the shaved heads, all seem to go together. It's a virile tough "look" that probably has its roots in prison survival. Some, but few inmates could be consciously emulating the military and the athletic. Military and athletic origins are survival oriented also, but not by appearance of toughness, but the actual need of not allowing an adversary to grab your hair while combating.

Shaved heads are obviously more expedient. No need no comb, clean or cut; no carrier of insects or disease.

The style of shaved heads starts in prison and army barracks but slowly becomes an esthetic style popular with the masses. Athletes and movie stars become the prototypes-types. Someday we will be a race of shaved heads! Baldness will be universal.

The law is clear and simple to those who read it.

California Civil Code Section 3537.
Superfluity does not vitiate.
Enacted 1872.

THE SO-CALLED LAW LIBRARY

The so called "Law Library", the sign being on the front of the facility – it being two long trailers fused together, with doors and windows added, is not really a law library at all. Every single law book and its quantity of law books is very small, is outdated and meaningless. Inmates do get copies of cases, mostly from the outside, do file pro per writs, do file grievances, write letters and fill out the numerous legal forms that are provided. There are ten typewriters in continuous usage.

But the bulk of the library is a hodge podge of general books, half hard bound, half pocketbooks, arranged into two sections, in alphabetical order. Books have been obtained from defunct libraries, and donated by the inmates who can receive them in the mail from the outside. Money for books, according to the librarian is annually appropriated for new books and supplies – $3,000 this year – but it is never actually given or expended for library needs. It's merely an accounting falsehood.

But the supply of books ranges from the secular to the divine, from Plato to cowboy westerns, from poetry to children's books. In general, it's not so bad for general reading.

Most of the inmates don't ever visit it; many that do don't really know the function of a library. Many think it's a social place to meet and talk. Others hide or sleep there. Many inmates horde books that they have read or intend to read. The limit for inmate's locker is fifteen books, but I've seen up to forty-five. Reference books are taken and kept by inmates.

When I first came, I placed the "New Yorker" current copy on the library shelf for all to read. It was taken in a few hours, never returned. I placed a new "Federal Prison" reference book in the law library portion, for everyone to use. It would have been a great asset to the inmates. It was taken by someone in one day, and never returned.

But despite the book thieves and the noise, many inmate academics, religious devotees, writ writers and scholars look to the library as a refuge and a place to think, write and read.

TRAPPING ANIMALS AT CAMP

Ground squirrels or prairie dogs abound on the outskirts of the prison camp. Their burrows are everywhere to be seen. They come out, stand erect on hind legs, look around like little scouts or sentinels. They eat the grasses and the plants; their underground tunnel system reaches to all parts of the camp. Their mounds of dirt appear on the camp lawns after night.

Brown weasels are the squirrels' predator. Their long tubular bodies fit into the tunnel homes of the ground squirrels. Their razor teeth find the victims.

Twice on camp grounds, I have seen inmates with caged weasels. Somehow there are cage animal traps here, presumably made by inmates for sport; they set the traps with food inside to entice the animals on the outskirts of camp, catching the weasel, then parading their catch throughout the grounds by putting the cage on the back of the batterized carts that are used for inmate transportation. The driver/animal trapper stops here and there, and the other inmates watch the frenzied weasel scurry about the cage.

I have seen the same traps used to catch the cats that populate and overgrow the camp grounds.

The cats are relocated, I believe; the weasels are freed after shown about. But the strange irony to me, unseen by the trappers and the admiring inmates, is the analogy between we, the prison camp prisoners, and the weasels and cats similarly incarcerated. We seem to pass on the cruelty perpetrated upon ourselves.

If we desire respect for the law, we must first make the law respectable.
Federal Maxim

PRISON LIFE WITHOUT MARIJUANA

It is well known that I am a marijuana activist. I have a doctor's recommendation to use medical marijuana and I espouse its use for physical and mental ailments. I smoke daily "outside," and have done so for approximately forty years. To my knowledge, I have suffered no detriments, and my physical being and state of mind has certainly been enhanced. All my trial lawyers role models have been alcoholics, so I am pleased that marijuana appears to me to mitigate stress without the ill effects of alcohol.

But in prison camp, I do not smoke. I terminated before entering like turning the page of a book. "How does it feel without it." "Want a hit" goes the refrain from inmates that know that I am a long term marijuana user. I tell everyone the following. Pretend that you have a garden of beautiful, multi-colored flowers. When I smoke marijuana, I can see a color, a gorgeous shimmering color, that no one else can perceive. The beauty of the secret flower's color gives me joy, pacifies my mind, provides stimulation to my imagination and bestows upon me a feeling of well-being.

In prison, I can readily suspend the viewing of this private esthetic wonder. There is no pain, no craving, no compulsion attached to the cessation of this conduit to enhanced perceptions and enriched state of mind. I feel the loss of the beauty, but I can reminiscence. I retain the memory. Memory is a sustenance for replacing lost beauty.

But marijuana is not a drug that addicts, enslaves, envelops the user. It simply enhances awareness. It increases one's appreciation of beauty and beauty is a component of truth and love.

Marijuana renders one with a more elevated state of awe. Abstinence does not enfeeble or destroy any portion of mind or body; it merely eliminates one blissful dream within the reality of one's life.

Thus I am very able to survive without marijuana in prison but one will see me smile, the idiot-savant smile of "flash-back" memories.

ABSTINENCE

There's no physical love in prison. It's the most singular meaningful vacancy in an inmate's existence. It is true privation. Celibacy is the death of a vital core of human life. The ramifications are profound.

No contact with your mate, no physical affection, no touching of flesh, no softness, no caress. A soft voice, a warm body holding, feeling, petting are all eliminated from the inmate's experiences.

Can anyone imagine how that destroys the balance between the physical and the emotional attributes of a man's personality? When love is missing, when no femininity enters into the male existence, there are a number of reactions visible at prison camp. Sublimation is one; over eating, over exercising, over sleeping, masturbation, pin-ups of sexual stimulating nature, porno magazines take the place of natural feelings. Homosexuality occurs in prison, but I think not at camp.

Hardening of the male psyche is another consequence of celibacy. The inmate becomes embittered, defensive, obscene in language and behavior, sexist in his pronouncements. The ability to be caring or to extend softness is lost. Depression, lonesomeness, isolation can also occur.

Why not furloughs home? Why not conjugal visits? Why does a society destroy the vital light of instincts to love and reproduction by inmates. Why are they eliminated from the "gene pool" of evolution? Shame on us.

A frivolous fear is not a legal excuse.

Federal Maxim

SOME INMATE SYNDROMES

Some inmates manifest what could be called psychological syndromes, or personality disorders, not serious but odd. They fall into several categories and a small but significant number of prisoners fall into each category:

1.   The super-cleanliness syndrome. There are a few inmates who shower constantly, one showers four or five times per day. Others or maybe the same ones wash their clothes constantly, after one, or an abbreviated day's wear. Some wash the same clothes twice in the washing machine to make sure they are clean. Many carry with them into the toilet and/or the shower a spray bottle of disinfectant (which can be purchased in the commissary), and spray toilet seat and shower stalls before using. These types seem to fear disease or contamination.

2.   Genital exhibition. Many inmates while in the dorm, walking about, or while talking to others, will have one hand down their sweat pants and will hold their penis or penis area openly, sort of a Michael Jackson gesture.

3.   Possessiveness. Some inmates become actually violent if you invade the space around their bunk – "their house" – or sit on their bed (while talking to them!) without first asking permission. One always asks permission to sit at the same table with other inmates when about to eat in the dining hall. When setting down your tray of food at the table, the inmate must be very careful not to take too much space on the table or bump trays with another inmate. An inmate was in fact assaulted (punched in the face) when he mistakenly took another's toast out of a rotating toast machine. He mistakenly took the earlier one. His was actually next. The bread was the same kind!

Two inmates coming from different directions arriving at a doorway at the same time must stop and tell each other to pass (by word or gesture).

It is taboo to cut anyone off, step into an already formed line, change TV stations, or borrow papers or magazines without getting permission. All inmates appear very sensitive – very "touchy" – on the above issues.

4. Hyper-vigilance. Inmates hide from the guards and administrators and avoid any contact at all with alleged informants. Constant watchfulness and signaling to others of their presence is universal behavior. Talking in whispers is common. One must always know where the nearest guard is located.

ETHNIC ADJUSTMENTS TO CAMP PRISON

Prison camp is a "melting pot" of races, religions and different socio-economic backgrounds. English, Spanish, Chinese, Philippine, Korean, Japanese, Iranian, several Middle Eastern and Ebonics are spoken here. The various ethnic and socio-economic groups self-cluster, but a generic fusion on many levels occurs.

As a consequence, generalizations about ethnic clusters or groups of inmates are fraught with potential error, but rough conclusions can be advanced.

The group that seems to have the hardest time adjusting to the regimented life of camp prison is the Hawaiians. There are many here, some doing long time. Most are large, tattooed, long haired, silent, sullen specimens. Maybe because they are used to outdoor living, under the sky, constantly in the sea water, free and mobile, the constrictions of prison are poison to their psyches. They walk around the dorm most of the time, shirtless, short pants, like on a beach, but seemingly dazed. They interact little, even with their own fellow Hawaiians. They sleep their time away. It's very sad to see Hawaiians locked up!

The group that seems to have the easiest time here are the Blacks. They are better able to live in the present. They socialize easy; they talk the street vernacular. They joke around, belly laugh, sing, cut each other's hair; many lift weights. They appear to have less escapisms than others.

The Hispanics, Asians, Whites and educated Blacks fall somewhere in the middle in terms of adjusting to prison life. Hispanics have strong ethnic ties. They speak the time to each other. They bond, they have church and family ties. They are the largest group in this prison! Asians, whites and educated Blacks react variably, but in general, they also self-cluster, self-segregate, read significantly, keep up with the outside news more dominantly, and plan for the future with more fervor.

The above generalizations are merely the untutored lay observations of this inmate!

FRIENDS LEAVE PRISON

In prison camp, we as inmates gain friendships with one another only to lose them. It's a process that happens on the outside frequently, but inside the process is accelerated. At a camp, inmates have relatively small time left to do before release. So bonding is temporary. You can be close, share life stories, work together, socialize, play sports together and the next month your new friend evaporates. He has been released or transferred to a half-way house. All say that they will come see you, visit, resume the acquaintance later, when both of you are out, but it seldom occurs, even for inmates who have been together for years. It's sad.

I have for nearly two months lost the friendship of several inmates with whom I enjoyed good conversation, prison information, social and political issues, legal strategies, home-life accounts. They come into my life and leave, and it in retrospect, seems like a dream.

Larry, the law librarian, the publisher of forty books on antique weapons, a great librarian, helpful knowledgeable. Roland, my inmate grounds keeper "boss." We walked the circle together. He was my "camp" teacher, he showed me the "ropes;" he gave me a newspaper to read each night; an old inmate from the "off shore" eastern islands, I was helping him with his writ; I knew his case. Bob, the guru of the mechanical repair shop, the oldest man in the camp, a guy who could fix anything. He gave me his "bath size" towel when he left. The smiling lawn mower man. He mowed. I watered. He shared his life with me: his "outside" life. An Indian-looking man from New Mexico, smiling eyes, strong charisma, loyal friend.

In less than two months, they all touched me deeply and then disappeared, released, gone. I'll never see them again, but they form bits and pieces of my memory forever.

California Civil Code Section 3531.

The law never requires impossibilities.

Enacted 1872.

ONE LONG DAY

Conformity and routine forced upon the inmate is the greatest intrusion into his freedoms. Prison life is led according to a fixed schedule. It's a slow but steady pace. It's the same each day. The clock is our taskmaster.

We rise at 6 a.m. Eat at 6:15. Clean our bunk area at 6:30. Report for job assignment at 7:30. Eat lunch at 10:30. Back to work at 11:30. Work ends at 1:30. Our count is at 4:00 p.m. Dinner at 4:30. Mail distribution at 5:30. Count at 7:00 p.m. Lights out at 10:30. Mandatory timed events – no deviation. The elimination of free will, choice, options and self-determination can turn a free spirit into an automaton.

It can be seen from the above schedule that there are allotments of so-called "free time." This free time for an inmate is a "camp" privilege, not applicable to real prison life. For instance, I do my writing from 6:45 to 7:30 a.m. I read and write from 1:30 to 4:00 p.m. I am relatively free from 6:00 to 10:00 p.m. I retire between 9:30 and 10:00 p.m.

But there are other necessary activities that must be done by inmates. Alleged educational sessions, medical appointments, the normal bathing, shaving, washing of clothes and sheets and towels; optional but consistently, the prisoner exercises, by walking, running, lifting weights, playing sports; the prisoner makes phone calls, writes letters, receives visitors, chats socially with his inmate friends. The time-constricted activities make days and weeks and months and years merge together. Prison time is like one long day, looking back at it.

To make laws that man cannot and will not obey serves to bring all law into contempt.

Federal Maxim

THE SICK, THE INFIRM AND THE INJURED

Inmates in general appear unusually strong and healthy. Resistance to penal captivity and threat of inmate assault brings bodily protectiveness to an apex. The posture of the virile male, the unbeaten, and the survivor is the image emulated by the inmate. "Don't tread on me" is the unspoken motto.

On the other hand, injury and illness do prevail. At the prison camp there's between 350 and 400 inmates stuffed into two barracks, beds cramped together, inadequate ventilation, mostly artificial light. It's inevitable that athlete's foot, coughs, colds and insomnia occur. It is said that sometimes the whole sleeping dorm is in unison with coughing and nose blowing.

The prison camp is set in rolling hills and valleys. Corn crops and cattle are plentiful. Bushes and trees are everywhere. Thus poison oak, allergies and skin rashes penetrate the camp. Some cases of allergies and poison oak are serious. Rattlesnake and spider bites infrequently occur.

Work assignments cause broken limbs. Several inmates are on crutches, wheelchairs and some with arm slings. They hobble in many cases around camp. Grave illness happens. Heart attacks and walking pneumonia have been seen here.

Although a "health building" (three rooms in a small construction) exists with a nurse present daily and recourse to doctors available, the sick, the infirm or the injured constantly complain about their medical treatment. Inattention, incompetency and indifference are the chief complaints.

Justice delayed is justice denied.

Federal Maxim

WORKING FOR FELLOW INMATES OR WORKING FOR THE PRISON

Lompoc Prison Camp is called a work camp. Everyone has a job assignment; no education, no rehab, just work. In general, inmates are disdainful and apathetic to their responsibilities. Work "faking" takes the place of working, and "hiding out" is the inmate's favorite activity. A five to six hour workday is the norm.

However, a distinction can be drawn with respect to the kind of work that is done; a distinction not readily acknowledged by the inmates. The difference is between working for the Bureau of Prisons and working for the betterment and comfort of the inmates: the former being penal servitude, the latter could be acts of comradery and mutual support.

Inmates who work for prison industries: the dairy operation (milk, cheese, beef) or the farm operation (corn, hay) are performing penal servitude, and an appropriate reaction could be resistance to such job assignments. These inmates are paid pennies per hour while the B.O.P. gains much revenue from their labors. Other inmates who are assigned to the kitchen, or clean dorms and bathrooms, who water plants and lawns or who garden or sweep in essence serve to enhance, to beautify, and to keep fellow inmates healthy and in a clean esthetic environment. This second class of job assignments directly benefits the inmate. Apathy and indifference to these tasks should be reconsidered.

While in the more synoptic view, all work in prison is for the government that has imprisoned us, it certainly feels better to do work that bestows a direct benefit on fellow inmates, rather than a profit to the prison.

California Civil Code Section 3526.

No man is responsible for that which no man can control.

Enacted 1872.

INMATE TO THE "HOLE"

One of the more harrowing sights at prison camp is the aftermath of a prisoner "rolled up" and sent to the "hole." Possession of contraband, failure to be present at count, talking back to a guard and a host of other infractions receive the sanction of being sent to isolation in the nearby main prison.

What's left of the inmate's "house," his bunk area, is what the other inmates see. Only the mattress and pillow remain. Everything else is taken by the guards, all of the blankets, sheets, pillowcase; the metal locker is put on a dolly and rolled away. The area is left stripped and naked. All of the inmate's possessions after being searched are kept in a storage area for his return weeks or even months later.

But the sight of the cleared out area, the instant realization that "Joe's" been sent to the hole, the vacant and empty personal spot of Joe, is a chilling sight for most inmates. We won't be seeing Joe; we won't hear him talk; we won't hear his laugh. We all feel lessened, deprived, diminished by the event. There's strong comradery in the barrack's dorm, and therefore, there is strong empathy.

Rumors spread like wild fire. "Joe got rolled up; what did he do? How long in the Hole?" The answers vary, maybe there was a witness, but most answers are speculation. Fear of informants spread with the hearsay. Soon the whole prison camp is abuzz.

There may be injury without any injustice.

Federal Maxim

MAIL CALL

"Mail Call 5 minutes." "Mail call 5 minutes." The camp P.A. systems blast out about 7 p.m. each night, Monday through Friday. The incoming mail is a much-anticipated nightly event for many of the camp inmates. We can receive and remit unlimited mails.

Whereas visiting friends and family and telephone communication is limited and must be approved in advance.

The incoming mail, other than "legal mail" from the inmate's lawyer, is always monitored, that is read by staff at the camp. It is opened and stapled closed after being read. No books or magazines showing nude photos are allowed. No photos of nudes are allowed. Nothing about explosives can come in. Outgoing mail is not monitored and remains sealed. Some inmates carry on extensive communications with people on the outside; they also receive commensurate mail.

When the mail call is announced, about one fourth of the inmates perform a nightly ritual. They line up in a narrow hall at one end of the dormitory. The hall leads to the front door exit, and entrance but also abuts the dorm's guard's office. The mail is distributed by the guard. It is done alphabetically. Both sides of the hallway are lined by standing inmates. The inmates waiting for their letter of the alphabet to be called stand face to face, talking, joking, some pensive. Three quarters of the inmates sadly do not come for mail. They expect nothing.

Some inmates come, not really expecting a letter, but hoping. The first letter of one's last name is called out from the guard's office by the guard, all "S"s for instance, rush into the small room. The guard calls out the last name as he sorts through the mail. It has already been stacked according to alphabet.

Some inmates get much mail, letters, magazines, and newspapers. Some get a single letter, looking like from a loved one. Some come away empty handed, hiding their disappointment.

Letters are carried back to the inmate's bunk, read while sitting on a folding type metal chair that each inmate possesses. Letters are read in silence. Memory is stimulated. Responses are thought about. Some write back immediately.

INMATE VICES AT A PRISON CAMP

The virtues and vices of the inmates of the prison camp perhaps are relativistic and subjective. But I enumerate below some of the vices that I see; maybe a better description, instead of "vices," I'll call them behavioral "traps."

The first that comes to mind is overeating. Food is the last sensuality available to the prisoner. Some inmates take huge helpings, stacks of bread, tray compartments jammed, over spilling with fried potatoes, cereal, and cakes. Extra helpings secreted to the sleeping dorm for nighttime snacks. There is an underground food service based on kitchen theft: stews, dried meats, fruit, rice and meat combinations are all available. The commissary offers canned sugar water drinks, candy bars, cookies and crackers. Some inmates gain weight; eating becomes their escapism.

Sleeping inordinately, oversleeping, afternoon sleeping, sleeping too early to bed at night; sleeping away the time, maybe dreaming, becomes another escapism. Sleep is denial. Sleep is the suicide of the mind.

TV, as the opium of the masses, is an addiction for many. There are three areas in the camp where multiple TVs are in place. Inmates bring headphones from the commissary to listen. They sit transfigured. They become the "couch potatoes" of the inmate population. TV habits are as chronic inside prison as it is outside.

Weight lifting is a peculiar prison phenomenon. The "irons" used to be present in most prisons, now only a few. At Lompoc camp there is a large outdoor spread of weight lifting equipment, from rowing devices to all forms of dumb bells. A large contingent of inmates spends all their free time on the weights. They become a race of their own: large, buffed up arms and torsos, usually with many tattoos displayed on arms and chests and back, even legs, distinguishes the body builder's breed. Prison can be tough and masculine symbolism is a protective device, but when bodybuilding becomes an obsession, and for many, it does, it can be a vice.

Self-segregation becomes habitual in prison. From my perspective, it's not a good thing: Blacks hanging out with Blacks, whites with whites, Hispanics with Hispanics, Asians with Asians, in the dorms, at the dining tables, at their leisure on the benches, in the gardens, in the TV rooms. They cluster together – Asian language, Spanish language, English language, all separated, many suspicious, some biased against the others. No "melting pot" in prison. The vice of reinforcement of social prejudices prevails.

The vice of apathy and indifference is ubiquitous. Because the camp is a work camp, the inmates are all given job assignments, groundskeepers, lawn cutters, repair persons, farm jobs, truck driving, warehouse jobs, sweeping, cleaning, all easy work. But a safe generalization is that inmates do not want to work for the prison system. This is not Siberia. As a consequence, most "labor fake," pretend to work, hold the broom, hold the shovel, make an appearance of labor. What occurs is that self-respect is lost; the work ethic is dissolved and apathy envelops the inmate's spirit.

A final (for me) form of damaging behavior, it's sort of a subjective vice, is the pitfall of self-victimization. It takes the form of whining and complaining, all the time, about everything, mostly petty issues. "The food is lousy, the guards are cruel, we're being exploited by having to work for the government, I'm innocent, the judge was unfair, the U.S. Attorney who prosecuted me is a liar, my wife left me, my children don't write." All the foregoing is true for many but obsessive complaining – "crying in one's beer" as the expression goes – is probably a sign of depression. It precludes a positive state of mind. It's boring to listen to, and is certainly an impediment to creative thought. I've seen that it leads to malingering too: "I have blisters, my shoes are too tight, they won't give me my medications, the doctor didn't even see me, my job is too hard on me." Like above, all of the complaints may be valid, but the vice is concentrating only on the negative, which disallows appropriate emotional healing. Many inmates do so.

California Civil Code Section 3542.

Interpretation must be reasonable.

Enacted 1872.

I AM A RAIN MAKER

The "real" Lompoc Prison has outdoor spaces between the old, decrepit, block-like steel-boned buildings, and between the buildings a double fence with curls of razor wire on top and in between. The outdoor spaces are flat, dry brown grass: nothing green no flower, no plants; a blanched, bleached downtrodden earth with deadened grasses, a threatening sterility, not of nature but defacing nature.

We shutter at the ground's bleakness when we pass in truck to obtain supplies.

Severely contrasting the prison grounds is the campgrounds, my abode for ten months. Our buildings and the entire compound are surrounded by lush green, well-mowed grass, with flowers, plants, cactus and bulbed protrusions. It is a camp within a garden setting, the pride of the inmate gardeners.

My position in the camp, my job assignment is to water, to flood, to wash, and to rain upon all living vegetable matter. I am the camp's rainmaker. I am the conduit for the life giving water supplied to the gardener. I turn on the sprinklers; I work the roses; I sprinkle the flowers; I inundate the growth with a steady stream of dancing, gurgling, spraying liquid.

I sing with water. I sow with hose. I am the maestro, the symphony leader with hose, not baton. I make music with my water. I am thrilled with my job assignment. Birds follow the path of watering. New life springs from the dazzle of the spout. It is almost religious to be a rainmaker in a prison camp.

LAST WEEK'S NEWS

In the life of confinement, we are beseeched by exaggerated self-interrogation. Most issues viewed from the outside would be considered trivial. On the other hand, many are philosophic. One such introspective challenge for me was whether nor not to say in touch with the contemporary news of the day, the chroniclers of daily history; to wit, whether to read or not to read the newspapers. Outside prison, I read two per day, the local paper and the New York Times.

Should I keep up with daily events; the war in Iraq, the government of Afghanistan, the prosecution of the American Corporate defrauders, the home run count of the famous baseball player, Barry Bonds? Why should I care? The Earth is not turning now for me. I am on a shelf; I have been warehoused. I will decry my banishment by disciplined indifference to the events outside my small microcosm of prison camp life.

Like many profound decisions, I decide to read old, belated, stale newspapers! Newspapers from the library, newspapers from other inmates, newspapers from the garbage cans: always outdated, antiquated, last week's news at best. It's akin to skimming a history book; it lacks the smack of immediacy, the call of urgency, the meaning of contemporary. It's safe reading, requiring no judgments, no alarm, and no emotion. I read the cold discarded leftovers of last week's occurrences, incomplete, scattered, and random. Thus, the "news" part of my mind is a speckled flurry.

There are not enough jails, not enough policemen, and not enough courts to enforce a law not supported by the people.

Federal Maxim

PRISON ESCAPE ON WIND

It's Saturday, a free day. I sit in the law library and read, read mostly of the pains and chills of ancient Russia, about the blizzards and the hunger, and I am warm and I am fed and the thoughts of privation are weightless on my mind, in Lompoc Prison Camp protected.

But outside the wind is roaring. Scant clouds flee, and raw air slams the eucalyptus trees, barely in my sight through a side window of the library. From hoarse shout to plaintiff scream, a windstorm spears the prison camp.

I look out; the wind is wiser than my book. Limbs and leaves fall in a flurry. The trees bend, shiver and slither under their attack. The leaves reflect light like flashing daggers hung aloft. I sit mesmerized.

Not prison wall nor fence, not law library building, not book, not vacant thought, can stop the wind. The wind is free and furious. It beckons to my liberation. It calls out from the freedom of its wings. It spills like madness on my constrictions. The gates are overturned; I flee from prison, soaring with the winds wildness.

I used to be very confrontational in certain cases and/or with certain judges and landed in jail for contempt on numerous occasions. I pride myself on the memory of being in jail for contempt in more jurisdictions and on more occasions than any other of my peer group. It has always been for me a positive experience. One of the earlier times involved a three or four day custodial confinement in a city outside of San Francisco. Because of the civil status of my incarceration, I was assigned my own cell, which is unusual. The beauty of it was that on one side, the Black Panthers who were in custody would bring me contraband food, hamburgers, things like that from the kitchen. On the other end, the Hell Angels-types would do the same. I was well attended, well fed, respected and held court with respect to their cases as frequently as they could make contact with me. On such occasion, I read and re-read much of Shakespeare and came out not only feeling brotherhood with the inmates, but advanced in terms of my literary intelligence.

INMATE GENEROSITY

The second night: In my bunk, hands under my head, looking up with my eyes closed, thinking here I am, who I am, feeling no pain, no dishonor, feeling graced, feeling my life-long abnormality. My peculiar attribute that living is good, things are positive, everything leads to some enlightenment, drifting from thought to thought, smiling inwardly that prison is one more step toward understanding.

I am reinforced by the generosity of the inmates. I am a "fish," a newcomer. I know nothing about the prison routine, about what personal items I will need. Inmate after inmate approaches me. Most do not know I am a criminal defense attorney. Most greet me as a stranger but they all have gifts: toilet paper, pens and paper, postage stamps, sweat shirts, extra socks, sweat pants, sweat shorts, a brand new prison jacket. The list is long! I am amazed at their comradery; their protectiveness, their alliance with a new prison inmate. The legal society "outside" is not like this. The "outside" is filled with rivalry and selfishness. Here, in the face of the common enemy, the guards, the prison authorities, the federal government, the inmates bond for common purpose. I'm told it's not so, in the "real" prison, but in the camp, all are supportive, friendly, helpful. We are a united cause. It's a strengthening feeling.

A slip of the tongue ought not lightly to be subjected to punishment.

Federal Maxim

DRACONIAN SENTENCES

Lompoc Camp Federal Prison is populated by countless "ancient" and youthful "mariners." Each has a story of misfortune that wrenches one's conscience. The circumstances of their cases, their sentences, their prison insults are given freely to each other. The inmates routinely examine each other's psychological wounds. Some, maybe most, accounts are exaggerated or fictionally accentuated, but allowing for a deflation of each grievance, there still remains abuse, dishonor and excessive sanctions, so much so that I, as a learned listener, not a naive one, stand shocked and outraged.

Young men facing five to ten years for slight offenses; old men having done dozens of years, older men who have given their lives to prison. "I got twelve years, and they didn't seize any dope." "I was falsely snitched off and I am innocent" and "I got sixteen years." "I took the beef for my brother, I'm in for nine years." "If I didn't plead, they would have indicted my wife." "I'm in on a conspiracy charge. I didn't know what conspiracy was." "I was left holding the bag, the others fled, so I was hit heavy." "I've done twelve years; my wife is still waiting for me." "I'm doing fourteen years, my wife left and is with another." "I have absolutely nothing outside waiting for me." "I'll never make it out alive, I'm too old." "They say I have a bad heart." And it goes on and on.

It is the dirge of the convict. It is their self-proclaimed funeral eulogy. It is an elegy of pain. It lies like a shadow over the entire prison camp: the excessive incarceration time.

The punishments do not fit the crimes. Retribution motives are misplaced. Federal guidelines for sentencing and mandatory minimum sentences are too severe, too inhuman. These camp inmates are no

45

threat to society. We torture them with these draconian sentences. No one should do over ten years in non-capital cases. We remain in the dark ages in our penal philosophy.

DINING WITH FELONS

We're fed three times a day here at Lompoc Prison Camp: breakfast from 6 to 7 a.m.; lunch from 10:30 to 11:30 a.m. and dinner from 4:30 to 5:30 p.m. There are about 350 inmates, so the "dining room" is always crowded. There is a long line outside waiting for the door to be opened, and then a long line of inmates inside waiting to be fed cafeteria style. Plastic trays and plastic spoons and forks are picked up while in line inside, no plastic knives.

The tables with four connected chairs are spread over the entire length and breadth of the room. The ambiance is always one of excitation. The food is satisfactory. In essence cereal or cream of wheat for breakfast; hot dogs, hamburger, and salad for lunch; pasta or rice with dabs of meat at night; always canned vegetables, string beans and corn. Occasionally an orange, banana or apple; always milk or coffee, tray-made cakes and plenty of bread. One can eat as much or as little as desired.

One sits at a space available. Many choose only inmate friends to sit with. I see racial clustering, but the norm is a fair mixture at each table.

The table conversation is animated, ranging from personal to philosophic. Everyone appears extremely courteous to each other. Food trading is common. For many, it is a high social event.

Abstractly, it is four felons at the table. Abstractly, it is four felons from different backgrounds convicted of different crimes, of different ages, different races, and different personalities.

The talk is intelligent, perceptive, self-revealing. Each person is individualistic. All are polite. The exchange of ideas is fluent. I learn from the dining room table talk adventure and misadventure, trivia and profundity. There is nothing mediocre. It is far more revelatory than its correlative on the outside where luncheons and dinners frequently have ulterior motives or hidden agendas. The repartee here in genuine. I much prefer dining at a prison lunch than dining outside with run-of-the-mill professionals.

THE CACTUS ON THE WALL

Every Wednesday morning a van picks up, in front of our barracks, the "grounds" crew to drive them to a remote area of the prison farm to do clean up and watering. I'm part of the crew. We bring our rakes and hoses. It's a few hours of work "off campus" so to speak. We are let off at the future site of a drug rehab facility: barracks and class-rooms for future use. It will house hundreds of inmates. They will be "taught" the evils of drug usage.

But presently the compound sits isolated, silent and foreboding. It is surrounded by well-cut and well-mowed cross lawns and fecund cactuses. It is a desert cactus haven. Huge artichokes, sentinel asparagus, quixotic shaped hands and, a thousand pins and needles, cactus of all shapes thriving in a prison. It's a cactus sanctuary. Tours should be conducted in this cactus garden.

I am brought by our crew leader, an older sunburned, kindly man, an inmate soon to be released, to a huge cactus growing up against the wall of one of the army-like rectangular buildings. He turns a faucet on nearby and winks at me. "I feed this one," he remarks. The cactus stands ten feet high, fifteen feet across; its multiple slices, looking like hand upon hand, joined and reaching in all directions possesses budding cactus flowers: an array of brilliant orange-red blossoms and scintillating sunset rays of light, like Christmas ornaments flashing for us. "These later on will be cactus fruit," he explains. "Many of us harvest and eat them. They are delicious."

Cactus flowers and cactus fruit: exotic, brilliant over-whelming. The plant symbolizes health, strength, well-being, and beauty. Its stickers are menacing, they protect the fruit.

I think to myself: "I will be like that cactus here at prison." There will be 'flower and fruit' within the barbed wire. I will seek it out within me."

49

California Civil Code Section 3527.

The law helps the vigilant, before those who sleep on their rights.

Enacted 1872.

LAWYER OR PSYCHOLOGIST

The inmates come to me with their hopes. I am a lawyer. They crave their justice. They want, some desperately, to be released. We talk about their appeals, and then writs and what can still be done. What issues remain? Are the issues still legally viable? What are their chances? They recite rote-like the facts of their case, the mistakes of their lawyers, the deceits of the prosecutor, the perjury of the witnesses. I listen attentively. I ask the routine questions. In what stage is the appellate process? Do they have a lawyer? Have they already filed one writ? What jurisdiction are they from? Who was their judge? What is their chief grievance?

I take everything they say with sincere earnest. I tell them I am not an appellate lawyer. My disclaimer falls on deaf ears. They need to believe there is a prospect no matter how thin, that they will ultimately be vindicated. Many assert emotionally their innocence.

Even when contra-indicated, when the reality is one in a thousand, I re-enforce, I administer optimism. I have not the strength of will to deny their hopes. The mentality of inmates, to think positively, to avoid despair and depression, to overcome bitterness and anger is more important than the truth of their legal situation.

California Civil Code Section 3532.

The law neither does nor requires idle acts.

Enacted 1872.

INTROSPECTION

The exterior features of the inmates manifest an almost amicable outgoingness: nods, smiles and greetings are the ostensible forms. The demeanors show interpersonal grace. "How's it going? What's up? What's new?" are the familiar chants. Knuckle to knuckle (with closed fist) bumping is the common "hand shake" equivalent. When an inmate leaves the dining table, the custom is to rap on the table his salutation of departure. To the casual observer, everyone looks socially extroverted.

But there is a deeper, sometimes darker, persona that the superficial greetings mask. All prisoners absorb themselves on deep introspective thought. There is so much inactivity that the window of their mind opens to them. Then they look at themselves inwardly, sometimes almost trance like. The inner life flourishes by the side of the outward appearances. In the line for meals, while raking leaves or serving chicken, while reading, while walking the loop around the prison camp, one sees the inward stare, the contemplation, and the random self-hypnotism of mental life.

We here in camp prison are drugged by our memories, our past life experiences, our loves and hates, all seen vividly daily in introspection.

I AM PAID TO GO TO PRISON

I always tell everyone: If asked, would I like to observe a fascinating who done it murder trial? I would respond "gladly." If further asked, would you like to ask the witnesses in the case a few questions? I would respond "of course." If finally asked, would you like to tell the jury what you think about the case? I would say excitedly "yes, overwhelmingly." Then I would become suspicious and ask my questioner, "wait a minute, how much do I have to pay to be so allowed?" The questioner responds, "Oh no, we will pay you to do it." What I'm saying is that being a criminal trial lawyer is so enthralling, I would pay to do it. I can't really believe that sometimes I am actually compensated for the great privilege.

I have the same attitude toward prison! The inmates are utterly unique. Prison is a "melting pot" of all races, religions, social and economic strata: all levels of education and very diverse life experience; large and small men; clever and dull men; wise and ignorant; thief and beggar, killers and holy men are all here at Lompoc Prison Camp. Not one is bourgeoisie. Not one is boring. Conversations in social settings outside prison are trite and mediocre. In prison, every story is the Rime of the Ancient Mariner. The inmates are risk-takers, adventurers, some of daring bravado, others with "steel trap" personalities. They are more physically fit, stronger and more individualistic than the norms outside of prison.

If asked, I would certainly pay to be here, to listen, to watch, to sometimes advise. I am immeasurably enriched. My understanding grows. I experience their outrage, their defiance. I feel their transgressions and their suffering. Each of them deserves a Dostoevsky novel.

The strange thing for me is that I have been given the rare opportunity, thus gift, to observe and to participate in the prison milieu, only upon the condition that I refuse to pay taxes. The government, in essence, has declared that I can be exempted from paying income taxes if I will participate in this rich, humanizing social experience of making observations, asking questions and drawing conclusions about the men in our prison system. I feel very fortunate.

THE DRUG OF COFFEE

In our sleeping barracks, my lower bunk is located on the main aisle that divides the room. Therefore, I'm about in the center. There's two barred windows with Plexiglas on either side of the building, both about seventy feet away from my sleeping spot. About 5:30 a.m., a grey light passes sparsely through each of them, and I awake. It's darkish. I rise. I obtain my plastic cup and stumble into the bathroom. There's a single, very hot faucet there. I fill my cup with the steaming water; drag back to my bunk area and open my locker. With a plastic yellow spoon, I place two spoonsful of "pure Columbian" instant crystalline coffee into my cup and stir. The liquid turns dark mahogany. I look at it. It's my morning splash on a sleeping mind.

I sip, I think, I feel my metabolism rise. Thoughts randomly spill out into my awareness. Bits of dreams of the night mix with law and home recollections. I think of watering duties for that day. I have notes on a piece of paper of things to write, ideas for later library endeavors. I become re-charged. Coffee is good for me. I thrive on the stimulation it brings. I drink coffee twice a day, at dawn and at dusk. Both times my mind is transfigured.

Coffee is my catalyst to alternate consciousness. Alternate consciousness is necessary to transcend the mundane form of life. I now excel. It provides the portal to critical thought. It is my present "medicine."

The prompt and vigorous administration of the criminal law is to be commended and encouraged, but swift justice demands more than just swiftness.

Federal Maxim

THE WIZARD OF REPAIR

About a mile away from the center of the camp, which includes the dormitories, eating building, camp administration buildings, kitchen, storage areas, Indian sweat lodge, visiting room and gardens, there exists a repair shop, several metal sheds, dark, dirty tools on the walls, a large pinup of a young provocative woman in a bathing suit, old chairs, and debris scattered on the floor. Outside various machines left by inmates to be repaired: lawn mowers, leaf blowers, washing machines, dryers, refrigerators, small battery run golf cart looking vehicles. All of the items to be repaired are used by inmates in various job related assignments. There is a chronic shortage of equipment in the camp so that repairs must be done quickly. Inmates wait for their implement to be restored for their usage. Coffee is drunk, conversation flows, motors turn, air pressure tubes sing out. The repair shop is a hub of life at the prison camp.

In the middle shed sits the inmate "wizard" of the shop. It's hot outside, full sun beating down. The wizard will not leave the coolness of the shed. His inmate assistants approach him for advice. He sits, never stands, and answers all questions. Occasionally a difficult repair is brought inside to him for personal handling. He is like a surgeon: tools are handed to him, oil can, and flashlight. As he opens the belly of the machine, all stand around and watch and learn. He mutters and swears but can fix anything, so the myth maintains.

He is the oldest inmate in the camp. He is 74 years of age, short, fat with still natural black hair. He is greasy. His clothes are dirty but he is a legend at camp. He is the wizard of repair and rebuilding of all machines. It is said on the outside, he was a very successful builder. On the inside, he is the mentor of the mechanics and electricians. His only spoken name is "Bob."

California Civil Code Section 3517.

No one can take advantage of his own wrong.

Enacted 1872.

A CAMP IS NOT A REAL PRISON

Let no one confuse prison camp with prison. It's like confusing purgatory with hell.

The horrors of prison are real: high fences, triple coils of razor wire, gun manned towers, yards of hard brown dirt, punishment and retribution, sadistic guards, prison gangs, frequent assaults, fear and intimidation. Camp on the other hand have no walls, no towers, green lawns, flower and cactus gardens, baseball, soccer, basketball, volley ball, horseshoes, educational classes, non-assaultive, non-gang oriented inmates. The stress level is subjective, where in the bleak dungeons of prison, stress is objective.

Camp inmates are selected because they are deemed not to be a flight risk, not to be a threat to their fellow prisoners, not prone to violence, disturbances or custodial crime. Really anyone selected for camp should be "outside:" home detention, ankle bracelet, or supervised release, working and being productive. Camp inmates are no threat to society. It is a waste of resources to have this intermediary "camp" level.

Camp inmates as a generalization have more "white collar" crime inmates then real prison. Many have succeeded and prospered in lawful activity in their private lives. They are leaders, interpersonally adept, educated and have been respected in their outside professions and careers. Camp inmates include many doctors, lawyers, corporate executives, finance experts, builders, contractors, people who could help other inmates with jobs and skills. It's an absolute waste of human resources to house this type in prison or prison camps. They should be made to work outside helping rehabilitation efforts as an option to prison.

A way of life that is odd or even erratic but interferes with no rights or interests of others is not to be condemned because it is different.

Federal Maxim

THE "PILL LINE"

Everyone in prison camp complains about the health service. One never gets to see a doctor, only nurses. Are they really nurses? Why are they so indifferent, unfeeling? Why do they think we are always malingering? There are no first aid kits available at workstations. Rattlesnakes are omnipresent but the camp does not have even one anti-snake bite remedy. Horror stories abound about inmates having seizures and heart attacks and are left in dire conditions, because no doctors are available.

Every new inmate, after about two to three weeks, undergoes a rather complete dental and physical exam, weighed, blood drawn for testing, blood pressure taken, skin examined for damage, history of operations or illnesses taken, and allergies noted. If anything is ostensibly wrong, the inmate is scheduled to see a doctor and medicines are prescribed, ointments distributed, work conditions ameliorated. Inmates do go to "outside" hospitals for operations, repair of broken arms or legs, cancer treatment, even for hip replacement.

The commissary supplies "over the counter" aspirin and other standard "pain killers" if one has the money on one's books to pay for them. Further, shampoo, hair conditioner, mouthwash, under-arm deodorant, toenail clippers and the like are available through the commissary.

I've watched the "pill line" form at 7 a.m. for medication dispersal by a nurse. The inmate goes to a window, shows his prison-issued ID card and is given his daily-prescribed dosage. The line is long and the procedure seems efficient. In short, "Health Services do not appear to be so bad."

Law ought to be in words, and words are utterly inadequate to deal with the fantastically multiform occasions which come up in human life.

Federal Maxim

NO ENNUI

I am in prison now! Stripped of duty and responsibility: ejected from my lawyer's life; from my family life; separated from my loved ones. No wife to touch, to talk. My routine asunder, indulgences gone, evaporated. To many, my reputation tarnished, to others a waste of time, an abandonment of purpose. I am in exile, isolated and rejected.

But none of the above touches me deeply. My vanity, my ego, my arrogance is impenetrable.

I have no ennui. I have no shame. Quite the contrary, prison is my plumage, my panache, a symbol of my dedication to a principle, to a belief. It is my distinction. I wear proudly the garb of a convict.

Lawyers serve so few ideals. We wear others' badges of courage and belief. We mouth other's ideas, and value systems. We validate client's acts of courage or defiance. We enforce others' revelation or cries for change or reform. We stand in other people's shoes. We walk behind them, not in front. We change horses to gain the share.

My peanut principle: "I will not pay taxes" has been my career banner held high. Tax is the plunder of the victorious. It is the price paid by the defeated. It is a tribute to the conqueror. The ruling class pays no tax, only the vanquished. In modern times, the working class pays. I am a free man. I will not pay their tax.

That is why prison is not for me the symbol of disgrace, the mark of lost salvation, a place for depression, a time of repentance or contrition. I exalt in prison. I am not here because of moral deficiency. I am here because of moral consistency.

So I find the prison life reinforcing. I find the prisoners fascinating. I read, I write and meditate. I have new freedoms now; freedom to think outside of legalese; freedom to find new vocabulary for goodness, beauty, love and honor.

65

I can be innocent again, idealistic and simple. I can thrive on romantic fallacy. I re-trench in sentiment, comradery. I am a man among men who have faced risk, danger and punishment, no common minds in prison, creative minds only. No bourgeois here. No "safe way" lifestyles, no cowards. I enlarge in prison. I do not diminish.

We here are all proud to be anti-establishment, anti-authority, anti-sheep, and anti-conformist. We are individualist. We rage at society's norms. We are the angry semantic fists.

Don't pity us. Pity yourselves.

INDIAN ROCK

A tall, blue-eyed Scandinavian-looking convict is the prison camp horticulturist, in specific, a master rose plant attendant, a gardener, a green thumb, a lover of flowers: strong, erect, pure and committed to adding flower beauty to the prison camp; in short, the felon of flowers. His sentence is still longish, for at least ten years he has created and tended the prison gardens. Prison gardens, mostly cactus and roses, are omnipresent on prison grounds. Thorny beauty, the image of the necessity of pain preceding, surrounding, protecting perfection and redemption.

This rose growing convict has become a monk. He enhances prison life for all incarcerated, whether or not the prisoner is aware or appreciative.

Rose bushes surround the visiting area here. The visiting area is under the eucalyptus trees, situated on much watered, much cut, well-trimmed, always green grass. Visitors are literally surrounded by a ring of full blossoming rose bushes. A family visit is so enshrined.

Under these same trees years past was Indian tribal existence. More Indians than whites now, once was located on this site. An Indian village once occupied the very location of the visiting circle.

The convict rose gardener in his digging of the earth here found a heavy, large, spherical block, obviously hand-hewn, carved and rubbed into a rounded artifact. Was it a symbol of Indian religious worship? Was it used to grind corn, crush acorns? How old is it? Where is it from? Its color is whitish. Two men are required to lift the near perfect sphere.

It has been placed within the rose plants. It has waves of light emanating from its orbit. It is the prison camp's "lucky piece." Inmates stop to look, to feel its grandeur. Families are brought over to see it. Religious people utter silent prayers to it. We all know at our prison camp that we are not exiles in oblivion. We know the rock is the center of our universe.

SWEEPING LEAVES

Here at the prison camp, everyone "works" goes the refrain. It's a "working camp," penal servitude. The booklet reads, "Prison is to punish, deter and for retribution." Rehabilitation, resurrection and reform are not objectives. A camp program speaker informs us that education of inmates is not a high priority.

So I wait for a job assignment. I'm a lawyer, so I'll probably be assigned to the farm to milk cows, my inmate friends sarcastically predict. Nothing here is efficient, logical or practical, it is said. Perhaps they want to instill a feeling of ineptitude, worthlessness; maybe it's a propaganda or conditioning device. The inmates say no, it's merely apathy.

Thus, before regular job assignment, I sweep eucalyptus leaves. Thank God for falling eucalyptus leaves. Five of us newcomers to camp ("fish") with large plastic rakes are placed under the eucalyptus trees, which line one perimeter of the camp. The trees are large and old, strong with many limbs filtering sunlight. Great arms of limbs and their hands of leaves reach skyward. Leaves descend always. Raking leaves is continuous and ongoing. We rake only a few hours a day. Labor at a "work" camp is symbolic only. It is a gesture toward real work.

But raking the leaves spreads the perfume of the trees to the earth. We stand in the crown of fragrance, our backs stooped, raking in the agreeable odors. We are bathed, refreshed, renewed by the scented dust that flies from the rake. It is the cleansing of our spirit.

MANDATORY CENSUS COUNT OF INMATES

It's mid-morning in the hub of the prison camp. That means for us about 9 a.m. It's been particularly chilly, and the sun has just cleared the perimeter of eucalyptus trees surrounding the camp's central structures. The spangled rays of sun warmth filter through the trees; my watering of the lawns in front of the sleeping barracks is becoming relaxing as the coldness dissipates and over the loud speaker, the prison guard barks, "Census count. Census count. Return to the barracks."

Such a command occurs infrequently. It means the camp administration fears that an inmate has escaped, and an emergency count of all inmates is mandated. Most inmates are away from the hub or center of camp, and they will also be counted at the sites of their job assignments. In such way, if there is an inmate gone, his identity will soon be learned. The process stops all work and takes about one hour. I run into the barracks and sit on my bunk, writing this account of the event. I leave five sprinklers running, puddles will accumulate; my hose lies unwrapped. The camp is quiet.

Inmates murmur in the barracks waiting to be counted by the guard. "They think someone ran away from the farm," says a voice. "I hope he's already in Mexico" says another. The guard walks by silently counting us one by one.

California Civil Code Section 3510.

When the reason of a rule ceases, so should the rule itself.

Enacted 1872.

ARRESTED FOR A CIGARETTE

Smoking has recently been banned at Lompoc Prison Camp. For more than thirty years, it has been allowed to the inmates and sold to them at the commissary. In specific areas designated "No Smoking" (like in the law library), signs are still present on the camp grounds. But presently, only the guards smoke legally and for the prisoners, it is forbidden. Cartons, packs and even individual cigarettes used to be the inmate currency of exchange, i.e., a pack of cigarettes for a haircut, three cigarettes for an apple, a carton for meal or laundry services. Now U.S. postage stamps and books of stamps have taken the place of the cigarette as the coin of the realm.

If an inmate is caught smoking, and inmates do smoke somewhat openly outside and in the rear of the camp, there are a number of possible sanctions. The usual are extra work assignments, washing camp vehicles or sweeping the dorms, suspended phone and/or commissary privileges, thirty to ninety days. Inmates are willing to risk the punishment, hand rolled contraband cigarettes are everywhere.

But just recently the reaction of the guards got more severe. A popular, young inmate athlete was searched at his job assignment area, and a few cigarettes were found on his person. He was handcuffed at gunpoint by two guards and taken to the "hole," i.e., isolation unit in the main walled prison. Arrested at gunpoint for a few cigarettes, taken away to a barred cell – INHUMAN – the inmates shudder.

California Civil Code Section 3528.

The law respects form less than substance.

Enacted 1872.

THE PIANO IN THE CHAPEL

At prison camp, in the grouping of buildings at the camp's hub, there is a chapel, a small building (nothing denoting religion on its outside) with three or four small rooms and one medium sized room with about sixty chairs facing a raised platform. A painting of a hawk flittering over a river valley of flower patches hangs behind the platform. There is a podium at its center and to its side, a small piano.

The chapel is multi-denominational. Islamic services on Friday, Jewish on Saturday, Catholic, Protestant and Buddhist on Sunday. The chapel is also used as an educational facility for the small number of classes given at the camp, and as a TV room, but these activities are weekday non-Fridays. Also, inmates on free time use the piano.

I frequently water the grasses around the chapel and listen dreamingly to the imperfect melodies emanating from the chapel piano. Even amateur playing gives delight to the untutored inmate ear.

Yesterday, an inmate friend of mine, a medical doctor of seventy-four years of age, confided to me, in disgust, that the Catholic priest "caught him" using the piano on a weekday, that the priest had forbidden him to use it; that it was part of the Catholic Mass, and that it could only be used by them on Sundays.

Thus, even the Catholic priest punishes the inmate; no piano for the inmate until Sunday Mass for Catholics only!!

On one of my tenures at the San Francisco County Jail at San Bruno, California, I occupied a single cell on the top floor. The structure and the confinement areas were ancient. The bars were rusty, the toilet odors were pervasive, and the shouts and screams of the inmates intolerable. The only asset which this old cell provided to its occupant was there was a high, thin window at the far end of the cell, looking out toward the grassy fields that surrounded the jail facility. Since I was on the top floor, the view was emancipating. The poignant image from that stay will always be the "feeding of the gulls." The gulls would swarm in about 5:30 p.m. and they would circle the back area of the jail like an Indian prayer dance. Many inmates were throwing pieces of bread out of the slit windows. They would catch them mid-air, flutter their wings, and fly to another location to devour them. All of us who participated smiled inwardly with glee that we had help feed such a free and wanton flying, curious life force: a bird on wing catching bread flung from jail cells! It was better than meditating. It was better than smoking marijuana. Feeding the gulls from the barred window at San Francisco County Jail is the metaphor of my life.

BRAIN ATROPHY IN PRISON

The mind is multi-faceted. Millions of antennas or sensors feed its functioning. It is stimulated from within undoubtedly, but also importantly from without, the empirical data filters through the perceptual apparatuses, the conduits of perception. Random and unexpected input enlarges and establishes new relationships with the existent chemical/physical status of the brain, and adds more meaning, complexity and understanding. We need the random input, the unexpected and novel perceptions. They impinge on the open sensitive nerve fibers and brain cells. Thus, new thoughts and relations emerge.

When life is dominated empirically (perceptually) by repetition and routine, where nothing new or unexpected is encountered, brain chemistry remains status quo, un-replenished, inactivated by the outside objects and events. As a consequence, the brain remains static and disengaged. Ultimately, the sensors, the antennas atrophy, dissipate by disuse, narrowing and diminishing of creative thought occurs. Simply put, the brain must be constantly fed through the eyes and ears, or it dies.

There is a school of pure reason where the mind is fed through an introspective approach, where all stimulation comes from the inside, i.e., thinking, meditation, memory, fantasy, analysis, etc., where everything necessary for mental growth can be obtained through inner self focus. But this view is too constricted. There is definitely empirical data to be perceived and accounted for by brain activity in addition to introspection.

Therefore, the deficit, the liability, the greatest penalty of jail or prison is the repetition without new and random empirical stimuli and the concomitant diminishment of brain activity. Brain enlargement by absorbing new data and creating new relationships to it, stops. The old brain data, lying in wait as a foundation for incorporating new information, unused, eventually withers away. Prisoners become in varying degrees, brain dead.

Also emotional experiences are required for brain health and growth. The brain chemistry reacts and accounts for emotions also. It goes without saying emotional experiences, i.e., feelings of awe, beauty, achievement, love, passion, exhilaration, joy, etc., are diminished in custody. Therefore, there is an appropriate diminishment of brain activity also for lack of emotional input. When there are no highs or lows of feeling in an inmate's life, where the normal panoply of emotions is lost, brain chemistry subsides and atrophies. Hence, boredom vanquishes the mind. Prison is more than incarceration of body; it is the demise of mind.

MALINGERING MADNESS

In a prison as well as a prison camp, there are always a few inmates who malinger, who pretend to injury or illness to avoid job assignments, to rest, to sleep, to obtain medication or who genuinely develop psychosomatic symptoms. Some will do it as a matter of routine. "I'm taking off tomorrow. I have a migraine coming!" I see inmates on crutches in the morning, playing basketball in the afternoon. I see inmates feigning insomnia to get prescribed sleeping pills.

But the strangest instance of all is the case of an inmate who recently has developed a so-called psychotic syndrome of mutely hours-on-end standing in place staring at the horizon. He stands solitary, erect, statue-like half the day in the hot sun staring blankly into space facing the distant hills that surround the prison camp. After his "standing and staring" period, he is altogether perfectly normal. We have ordinary discussions at breakfast, lunch, dinner and the evening hours.

When asked, what's he doing, he says that he was being over-worked by the federal guard at his job assignment, that he only has a few more months to go, that he has been sent to a psychiatrist who agrees with his strategy, and that he listens to music via ear phones while standing, so it's not so bad. So is he mimicking madness to get out of work or is mimicking madness a form of madness? Whatever the diagnosis, he is a camp "yoga" symbol now.

LAST VESTIGES OF SENTIMENT

There are many hard, tough, cold inmates here; inmates who have been "down" ten to twenty years, inmates who had to emotionally freeze themselves in a shell of virile self-protection. They emit no joy, no compassion. They have voided themselves of empathy and sentiment. It's a sad thing to see.

So it's a purifying breeze when one sees some small symbols of sentimentalism, the undying image of humanism in a prison environment. Let me share a few:

The inmates at camp are very solicitous of the well-being of sick or injured co-inmates. The injured or sick in wheelchairs are wheeled around, everyone talks with them. They are wished speedy recovery. Others procure their meals for them. Their needs are taken care of, their clothes washed. This is also true for those on crutches and especially for the blind inmates here at camp. Instead of "chicken-pecking" the weak and infirm here at camp, survival of the fittest means survival of the weakest.

Another "soft" prison camp symbol is the posting or scrapbooks keeping of home and family photos. Every inmate plasters the insides of the metal cabinet, near one's bunk bed, with magazine photos of pinups, many being very sexually alluring. The cabinet doors are about 5 feet by 2 feet. So many photos or pictures can be taped to the inside of the two out-turning doors. Many inmates, buffed up weight lifters included, post photos of their wives, their children, their home and their parents. They stare at them at odd moments lovingly. They nurture their continuing affection for their family. It's their last light in a long dark tunnel.

I receive, on a relative scale, much mail. Many cards and letters have unusual and beautiful stamps. I have received foreign origin letters and cards with English and Chinese stamps on them. One inmate, thin, bearded and unkempt, in the peripheral of inmate society, told me that he has a child who is a stamp collector. I have given him every unusual stamp that I receive, so that he can send it home to his child. He is very appreciative. He brings me gifts of radishes and cheese. I do not accept them, but I take pleasure in his happiness to be able to provide something meaningful to his child from prison.

THANKSGIVING AT PRISON CAMP

Thanksgiving Day in a prison camp; it's a holiday. Breakfast, cereal, cake, apple and coffee were served at 7 a.m. rather than the usual 6 a.m. Many inmates stay in bed, sleeping, dozing, and reading until count at 10 a.m. I eat, I throw water on my face, I put on my green uniform and I go to the library. Not many inmates will wear their green uniforms today. Most wear commissary bought gym suits, grayish white. Uniforms of prison do not have to be worn on weekends or holidays, but I anticipate a visit from Vicki. I don't know if she will really come and visit or not, but I wear the required uniform for visiting just in case.

There is a so-called Thanksgiving feast planned for the camp at regular lunch time of 10:30 a.m.: turkey, real turkey, not the pressed, hydrogenated, "preserved" turkey roll slice that we get here on occasion, but real turkey and the side dishes common to Thanksgiving. Many inmates are excited about the prospect. I don't value food much; and further, if Vicki comes, I'll be in visiting and will miss it. They will only serve the big lunch today. I already picked up a "bag dinner," given out by the kitchen. Such will be my only food today if Vicki comes.

The weather promises warmth and sunshine. I put my sun block on my nose and cheeks, because if Vicki comes, and if we are lucky enough, we will sit outdoors in a visiting circle, surrounded by flowers and eucalyptus trees, and in the sun, maybe for three or four hours. I do give thanks for sun today: spring sun in winter.

I think, what do I have in my personal life to be "thankful" for: certainly not our government or prison. Our country is going totalitarian, and we are in endless war. Corruption in business and government is rampant.

But I have Vicki, the children, all doing well, good friends, my lawyer allies; I have my career flourishing, just got a good article on it in San Francisco Magazine, will have an article in California Lawyers Magazine next month. I still have my license, and most of all I have my health it appears and my physical and mental strength.

So from prison, I say, Happy Thanksgiving.

A PEACH IS A SACRAMENT

"My kingdom for an orange," I used to remark to fellow inmates the first few months of incarceration when they asked if I needed anything. At Lompoc Prison Cap, fresh fruit is a rare luxury. What is procured by food services goes underground and is distributed like drugs for appropriate consideration. I don't participate in the contraband food system so an orange or pear or peach is a treat as well as needed nutrition. Everyone knows that I help as much as I can with inmate legal problems so that on many occasions I am the recipient of a gift of orange, banana, or peach. Oranges are out of season now, so currently I receive from fellow inmates one or two peaches.

They come to me unripe and hard. I hide them in my locker under a spare white baseball cap. Frequently, there is a locker search and contraband items removed. It takes about four days for them to ripen. They are middle-sized peaches, rosy red and crème colored. The flesh under the skin is orange. They are juicy and sensuous. In the afternoon after standing four to five hours in the hot sun, I come in and devour clandestinely the peach. The flavor impacts my taste buds with explosive force. The juices spill down from my lips. It is a lush stimulant to my physiology and psychology. I feel the vitamins buoying my health. For me, the peach is a sacrament. It connects me to the gracious life-style of the free outside.

Nothing is so opposed to consent as force
and fear.

Federal Maxim

SURVIVAL OF THE FITTEST

Survival of the fittest in prison means survival of he strong and selfish much of the time. It is observable that survival of the "species" is a theme of incarceration. It's the patent self-clustering of various groups, racial, ethnic, economic status, degree of education, bikers, truckers, etc. These self-segregations are openly for purposes of self-protection and self-betterment. Such easily fits the principles of Darwinism.

The purpose of this comment, however, is not the above. What is seen collateral to "species" survival is personal, selfish survival tactics that serve the individual only, sort of ultimately anti-Darwin.

The most obvious is that the larger, the stronger get first choices, first pickings on everything issued. They can step in front of the food line; the TV room spaces are theirs for seating choices; the better prison blankets, inmate clothes, even in job assignment choices, they are given priorities. The next type is the "quick" in line, running to be amongst the earlier arrivals at TV, movies, food, etc. It's almost repulsive to see an inmate at the head of the food service line to take multiple fruit (I have seen one take a dozen apples), all the milk left over from breakfast and extra helpings, which ultimately deprive the last segment of inmates in line of their fair share.

On the grounds, prevailing by de facto theft is commonplace. Removing tools, water hoses, even flower plants, especially rose plants from one section to the inmate's section of assignment allows the thief to "do better" at his assigned task to the detriment of the others section's inmate. In the dorm, theft of clothing, blankets and food is common. The stronger and the more audacious are louder, inconsiderate of the privacy or sleep of the weaker. Weakness or age has no prerogatives.

Even in the library, books and magazines are illegally "taken out" and not ever returned. They are shared by the thief's friends. The librarians use the library as their social club, eating and talking incessant, in full view of their posted sign saying "no eating, no talking and quiet."

In short, in prison life, the survival of the inmate and the inmate's cluster "group" is of paramount concern. Unfortunately, to the weaker and to an outsider, the conduct at times seems unduly selfish and self-centered. The real "species" to survive here should be all inmates, not merely the strong and the stealthy.

WHEN A DOOR CLOSES, A WINDOW OPENS

I know that it is over-simplification but what I'm observing about my mind's operations is that the multi-faceted components of the brain are like body muscles that atrophy with non-usage. If you don't use a part of the brain, you lose that part of the brain as the platitude goes.

In prison life, one has no control over the "where" and the "what" of body behavior. That is, the prison routines are enforced, repetitive and become automatic. Where the inmate will be and what he will be doing is prescribed by prison authority. The prisoner lives an external existence of scheduled behavior: lights off, sleep; lights on, awaken; breakfast, work assignment, lunch, work assignment, library, exercise, dinner, reading, writing, lights off again, day after day; nothing random, no surprises; the camp routine over and over again, until we all expose only a mechanical robot mentality with regard to our ostensible activities.

When there is no choice, no alternatives, no options in regard to daily actions, that part of the brain that connects, bears nexus to and regulates and responds to external behavior, diminishes and disappears ultimately. Where there is no requirement to respond or react to the unexpected, the random or the spontaneous, the need for pragmatic or innovative thought and ideas evaporates.

Thusly, that part of the brain that is utilized in addressing the random, the unexpected, the unknown becomes victim of attrition: not merely brain reactions to change of physical movements, i.e., running, jumping, dancing, sitting, standing, but more significantly, the ability to vary attitudes, responses and judgments of the external environment. Inmate greetings become meaningless and rote, attitudes become collectivized, judgments repetitious and stereotyped. No challenges equal no creative thoughts equals mindlessness toward the imposed order enforced on the inmate.

For many, when the door to innovative thought closes, the window to a rich and varied inner life opens. The innovations, the random images, the assimilation of ideas, the synthesis of ideologies, the examination of psychology and philosophy, the ability to formulate mental options and choice of thought subject matter become the inmate's primary landscape of awareness. This is all internalized.

What appears robot-like on the "outside" countervails an ever-increasing, creative complexity of thought prevalent "inside." As one form of brain component atrophies, other new brain components emerge!

THE "POSSIBLE" FOOD RIOT

There is an Air Force Base next to our prison camp. Occasionally at night, we see the comet-like trail of splendor streak from a rocket shot out to space; we frequently see huge four jet transport cargo planes closely overhead as they decline for landing at the base airfield. Jets flashing by are regular.

About twenty inmates are job assigned to assist the clean-up and maintenance of the air base. The air base is outside of the perimeter of the camp. The inmates are driven out of our facility each morning, complete their workday, and are driven back in the late afternoon. The Base is about a one-hour drive from the hub of our camp. As a consequence of the distance, bag lunches are prepared by the kitchen and delivered to the inmate workers each lunch meal at about 11 a.m. Ninety-five percent of the remaining inmates at camp eat at the dining hall cafeteria style. The dining hall luncheon meal always contains something cooked, either warm or hot. Frequent lunches feature a main entrée of chicken, hot dogs, cold meats, and scrambled eggs. Sometimes we have fresh milk, sometimes an orange or apple or banana, many times rice and beans, bread or tortillas.

The bag lunches for the Air Force crew are far less replete. I am assuming mostly cheese, baloney or peanut butter and jam sandwiches with fruit and perhaps salad.

At any rate several of the Air Force assigned inmates felt, probably realistically, that the bag lunches contrasted to the kitchen cooked hot lunches were inadequate.

We, at camp, are allowed to present complaints via a form to the administration. The form is called a "cop out." These "cop out" forms are readily available at the camp officer's office, or the library. They are used constantly by the inmates, although most grievance requests are denied.

About four or five of the base-assigned inmates filled out "cop out" forms separately, complaining that their lunches were deficient. When the complaints were received and considered by the administration, each inmate who had complained was promptly arrested. They were "rolled up," their bunks and possessions taken and they were placed in the main institute outside of camp, in locked down isolation. We call it "going to the Hole." They remained there for nine weeks as punishment. Their infraction was designated as inciting possible food riot or food strike.

I saw them when they were released after nine weeks back to the camp status. They looked wane, fearful and agonized. They and all others who know about their treatment will never complain about the prison food again!

Such is the way the inmate is intimidated in prison against asserting rights and making just complaints!

ANOMALIES

Prison camps are populated with the so-called American outlaw, i.e., people who are convicted of crimes that someday will not be crimes, or prisoners who will be the folklore heroes of future generations: the marijuana farmers, the smugglers, the tax resistors, the political demonstrators, even those caught in the over-expansive net of conspiracy law. Convicts are thought to be strong willed, high risk, courageous, defiant, individualistic and self-determined. At least many fall into this media stereotype and in reality, many are of such attributes.

However, in prison camp, the vast majority are followers, not leaders; conformists, not independent thinkers or conventional, not creative. While all appear anti-government, and are so in their personal prison lifestyle and belief system, they behave like non-thinking sheep for the most part.

Status imagery is very important. Fashions and styles of appearance dominate: "pressed" prison uniforms, white tennis shoes, shaved heads, weight lifters bodies and tattoos are epidemic. Most inmates groom themselves to "look alike" in these particulars.

Language and gestures universalize: "Hey, dude," "mother fucker," the fist bump handshake, a knuckle-knock on the table when leaving from chow, walking the dorm like parading wrestlers, much talk and swagger repeated and copied by the inmates.

Inmates feed on rumor and hearsay. Every bit of gossip is passed around thrice. It's never critically evaluated, always taken as the true account. What movies to see, what TV shows to watch, what radio hosts to listen to, what books to read – all such past times are dictated to the masses of convicts who line up to conform to the norms of entertainment, and later discuss it ad nauseum: sheep mentality to an outsider!

Values are likewise inculcated by the inmate population and for the most part, adopted uncritically: who's the best outside soccer player, baseball player, what is really happening in Iraq, or the motives of this Republican Party. Individual thinking on such subjects is rare, all accept the prevailing view, reiterate the same trite formulas.

Contraband food is best, talking loudly is admired, cursing is respected, complaining is revered, the silent, the intellectual, the "thinkers" are held in lowest esteem.

It is sad to see inmates turn to sheep in custody, when outside they seemed so strong.

INMATE SHARING

I was issued two used towels, small, thin ones about eighteen inches by thirty-six inches, what on the "outside" we call hand towels. I do laundry once per week so that the towels are used about three times each per week. They are not large enough or dry enough (after first use) to really do the job. But recently an inmate that somehow possessed a thin used large bath towel gave it to me because he is to be released in a matter of days. Such is the custom – exiting inmates give away their issued possessions. I now can dry myself after shower in a more complete manner.

Such is the tradition here at Lompoc Camp Prison, the giving of personal possessions when a new inmate arrives and upon the release of an old inmate. Soaps, shampoo, towels, coffee plastic mugs, stamps, newspaper and magazine subscriptions, pin-up semi-naked woman's photos, pencils and pens, vitamins and aftershave lotion – everything is passed on and on. It's an ongoing unifying ritual.

I have received the best and the worst from fellow inmates: a sweatshirt – brand new with hand pockets (a rarity, the envy of many) was given, among many items from many prisoners. Also a pair of old worn beaten slippers, also noticed by many of the inmates because they're one of a kind here and because they are so bedazzled.

I know that sooner or later, I will also pass on the bath size towel. It's like handing off the baton in a long distance race to the next runner!

During a jury trial on one occasion, a defendant was allowed to bring a very fancy cup of tea, kind of like English-style with a saucer, into the court and drink during the proceedings. I don't know how or why the court allowed it but it did occur! It was much later after the trial was over that I learned that it was methamphetamine, not sugar that had been stirred into the tea!

THE COFFEE CATALYST

For many, inside or outside of prison, one must step aside or stand above their life's events in order to more clearly "see" themselves: see themselves in relationship to their environment, in interpersonal relations, to discover their true value system, in essence, to better understand themselves more objectively.

To obtain that "outside" perspective, or that transcendental point of view, many persons have resorted to triggering an alternate consciousness or alternative awareness. It's a relativistic and subjective state of mind. Many can obtain alternate consciousness by meditation, by yoga, prayer, exercise and running - also by consuming legal and illegal drugs. "Psychedelics" open portals to mind. LSD, mescaline, hashish, even marijuana can provide the synoptic point of view for the user. Many famous writers and poets have been opium users and many others alcoholics. Drugs can provide the creative insight.

In prison, for me, as a garden waterer, the long standing in the hot sun, holding of water hose spraying droplets of vapor, streaming rays of water toward the earth allows for a dream state that is a form of alternate awareness. The mental imagery is surreal and random, some retrospective memory, some sparks of interpretation, logic, law, fantasy, and realism co-mixed with imagination.

But the greatest antidote for tedium in my prison life is a cup of hot instant coffee. Maybe because prison routine is so repetitive, and therefore, boring, the mind throbs more dull-like, so that when a jolt of hot caffeine strikes the mental chemistry, the ensuing stimulation seems more intense than actual.

But coffee facilitates mental processes; it allows focused linear thought. It provides a facile mind mechanism that readily assimilates data and articulates relationships and causalities. I think faster; I

97

write more; I feel elongated (not necessarily like on "psychedelics," enhanced or enlarged) and automatically seem to probe multiple dimensions of a single issue.

I think I have become an inebriate of coffee (but I only drink it two or three times per day). I wait for the rush, the clarity, and the energy that it provides. I guess that there is always something that people find that has a transfiguring catalytic effect for them in producing the so-called alternative consciousness.

I SEE NO CATS ON PRISON GROUNDS

"Fuck the rat who snitched me off." "Fuck his father." "Fuck his mother," an inmate in a wheelchair screamed the foregoing to a large watchful gathering of approximately fifty inmates and a dozen guards. He had been just taken into custody. An outlawed cell phone was found somewhere on his person or in the wheelchair he used. He was paralyzed by a "drive by" gunshot while on the street. He knew that a "rat" had tipped the authorities of the whereabouts of the phone. The guards circled him while he screamed his epithets but did not touch him. The inmates froze in awe. He was thereupon wheeled away, headed for the "hole," i.e., isolation cell punishment.

The guards of that hour remained, and as all inmates had been ordered out of the sleeping barracks, they searched each of us, and then searched all inmate lockers. The phone incident became a dormitory "raid." Dogs were brought in to also smell for drugs. It was a law enforcement show of force; it was overkill for a simple mobile phone contraband arrest.

Later that afternoon, while watering, the normal camp administrator asked me if I had seen any cats around the grounds. They wanted to trap and remove all stray cats on the compound. I knew where they were located but with "fuck the rat" still ringing in my ears from earlier that day, there was no way that I would inform on anything, not even a cat!

ANOMALY IN PRISON

Anomaly is the general rule in prison camp: from the physical to the ideological. In the physical realm for me, I eat food that I would not consider outside: cheap hot dogs, sweet cereals, cold cuts, white rice and endless canned vegetable and fruits. I go to bed regularly; I rise at the same time each morning and I receive mail at mail call time. Outside my life is irregular; inside it conforms to prison schedule.

But the strangest abnormality for me is my choice of inmate friends. Outside my associates and intimates all share my general social values: pro-working class, anti-materialistic, egalitarian-oriented and anti-government. But inside, I have gravitated to those who are semantically oriented, those who are knowledgeable of world events, those who have traveled; in essence, and those who have been acculturated by education or experiences similar to my own. But oddly the ones that I have found in this category are all committed capitalists: a doctor who owns a chain of diet clinics in the Los Angeles area; a New York mortgage banker multi-millionaire; a tax lawyer with a huge second home on an estate in Idaho and a hard drinking land developer from Lake Tahoe.

Money drives them all. Opulence characterizes their possessions and lifestyles. They are all victors in the capitalistic world of economics. But they are hip to the prison system fallacies and contradictions; they revel in ridicule of the guards and camp rules. They have the last minute news on Iraq or Israel and Lebanon; they have read and traveled and are cultured and worldly. Our discussions are animated. We share our past anecdotes and humor. We have bonded. We are known as the "gray power" clique (club). They know my opposing social philosophy, essentially Marxism, but such doesn't seem to deter our friendship. I strongly believe that on the outside, we will revert to having "nothing in common," and never see each other again.

I feel badly that the inmates that constitute the class I've always represented, the drug outlaws for the most part, who are abundantly present herein prison camp, I still serve when called, respond when queried, talk to frequently but abbreviated, am friendly with but not close, not sharing thoughts and ideas like the others that I have herein mentioned. It's because for the most part, they are not well read, well-spoken or keenly articulate. They are average minded with average world experience, not so interesting at a personal level contrasted to the rich successful capitalists!

SAGA OF A CHICKEN LEG

The rumor is that tons of frozen chicken legs were dumped on the Bureau of Prisons. As a consequence, we have baked chicken legs once or twice per week. It tastes okay; most inmates like it. It comes hot with a bottled barbeque sauce spread sticky over its skin.

It's a well-established understanding that everyone who works in the prison camp kitchen, inmates and guards appropriate food. It's against the rules but it's de facto legal. For instance, the kitchen receives fresh tomatoes, cucumbers, broccoli and much more that the kitchen never serves the inmates. It is taken, passed on and ultimately served in the clandestine underground inmate food service. Half the inmates at camp eat not at the dining hall all of the time, but in the gardens, at their bunk, and eat of the private inmate cook's offering.

Thirty dollars a month buys all meals underground. Stamps are the medium of exchange inside, but outside money is sent from family to family of the inmates. Most of the food served underground is spiced, diced, and mixed with rice or served Mexican style in burritos. Some of it is good, some is mediocre but it is the forbidden fruit (that really is allowed) so it tastes much better than the prison-cooked menu.

Obviously the frozen chicken is a main staple in the underground inmate kitchen. Barbequed legs or pieces in rice or beans are common. It really, to me, tastes the same as what the prison cooks, but it provides an alternate economy to the inmates. Because inmates prize the experience of furtive eating, they pay for it. The one who provides the raw food gets something; the one who transports it gets something; the one who cooks it gets something and the meal distributors get something. The alternate food system is like drug dealing. Everyone in the chain from acquisition to distribution participates in the profit of the enterprise.

The inmate ultimately eats the same chicken leg as the prison prepares, but it tastes better subjectively, and supports a large segment of inmate population. Therefore, stealing chicken from the kitchen is a good thing; even the guards look the other way!

DAYDREAMING – OPIATE OF PRISON

Although at a prison camp there is very little physical isolation, in fact, it's hard to find a lonesome spot, one's constantly surrounded by men, voices and activities. You find ordinarily you're in a sound studio of maddening chaos. But there is for every inmate, hours and hours every day of inward reflection. The routine, the boredom, the tedium of prison existence opens portals to scrutinized memory, ideas, beliefs, childhood, growing up, schooling, sports career, family. Every conceivable pocket in your memory is elevated to consciousness and examined. Musing and daydreaming are the opiate of the inmate.

Lying on your bunk, sitting, reading in the library, looking up from your book, while hosing the lawn, while raking leaves, while walking the grounds, while sitting staring off into the hills and dales of the topography, one sees the glazed stare, the introspective focus of the daydreamer.

Inmates and probably only a few other categories of people have this luxury or vice, depending on how one sees it, of "dead" time in which to visit your inner thoughts. Thinking about your past, the "fun" you had with your brothers, the time you won the one hundred yard dash, or made the touchdown, your early romances, your special achievements, the mind tricks you. The healthy mind rationalizes everything. For me at least, reliving the past in prison is "all good" as they say here.

But the most extraordinary aspect of recollection sessions is that you sentimentalize the episodes, the relationships, the events of your past life. Tough, burly, long-term prisoners stare back at themselves with tears dropping inside of them. You romanticize your loved ones, you glorify your accomplishments, and you become intoxicated on your self-reverie.

I am proud to say that I represented Hells Angels Motorcycle Club members for approximately fifteen years on all variety of charges including a federal racketeering case in San Francisco. I learned to admire and respect the Hells Angels. They, for me, are like the western cowboy outlaw image of the 1800s. They are ruggedly individualistic. They prize freedom. They uphold constitutional values. They are literally poetry on wheels. During the racketeering charge, I represented a major defendant who was later acquitted! At that time my children were young and we all lived in a little seaside hamlet called Bolinas just north of San Francisco. One of the cherished memories I have are the Hells Angels with their pounding, rhythmic motor sound coming to this little town, putting my children (I had five of them) on the backs of their motorcycles and spiriting through the paths and roads of the vicinity. It was fabulous for them; it was fabulous for me, even now!

INMATE MASCULINITY

Masculinity posturing permeates a prison camp. It's an instinctual survival technique. Regular walled, barbed wire, fenced, towered prisons are classified into degrees of security from, in essence, maximum to minimum. Each level of security rising to the maximum has a commensurate level of stress for the inmates. The most stringent, harsh levels house the violent, the gang members, the assaultive, sometimes even psychopaths.

In the inmate population of the non-camp prisons, might makes right, force rules, and intimidation is the control mechanism. The inmates need allies to align with for self-protection. Inmate extortion, rape and theft are norms. The strong survive; the weak perish. Thus for self-protection, every inmate must be tough or look tough. Shaved heads, tattoos and bodybuilding are the methodology.

At a prison camp, even though the assaultive inmates, the gangs and the violence do not exist, many of the prisoners come from "inside" as the "real" prisons are referred to. Thus, the camp manifests the same Machiavellian imagery. There really are an inordinate number of huge, giant-like men, tall, muscular, tattooed, showing biceps bulging from the weight irons. They wear armless tee shirts at free time to show off their muscles. They set the tone for the inmate to emulate. Eighty-five percent of the inmates workout, shave their heads, march around with their chests puffed out, swagger their virility. Understand a prison camp is an all-male environment. In some ways it's like a pack of suppressed wild dogs, wild thoughts, and wild instincts. It's classical natural selection, survival of the fittest.

To survive, at least psychologically in the camp, the inmate must curse, employ vulgarity, openly demonstrate hostility to authority, coalesce with comrades, and above all give the appearance of readily available combat prowess. One's masculinity puffed up to its highest point is one's security.

In the sixties and seventies, boat loads of Thai stick marijuana were in plentitude in the Bay Area. We had all forms of vessels smuggling in this highly rated sacrament. The Thai stick was certainly one of the innovations of the East that fertilized the minds of the West! In one particular case which I will remember all my life, I visited with a client in the Bangkok Jail facility. The visiting place was at the end of a building, one story high with a large barred window. In front of the barred window on the outside was a moat, and the moat was at least fifteen feet wide and had water in it. The lawyer is not allowed inside the jail. The lawyer stands on the other side of the moat and screams fifteen feet to the incarcerated defendant who stands at the window behind the bars. Everyone circles around to listen. This is their version of a confidential communication between client and attorney!! So I will never forget screaming out the questions that were to be answered and soliciting the answers as a precursor to the trial.

RULE BY FIAT

Tyranny by arbitrariness prevails in a prison system. To control inmates, they must be kept in a state of "unknowingness." The administration cannot allow prisoners to predict the judgments, conclusions and policies dictated by the guards or administrators. If the government's opinions, conclusions, reasons and directions to inmates were of a definite pattern or design, and thus government behavior could be inferred, the government could be manipulated and their control compromised. Thus, "keep them in the dark or keep the inmate guessing" is the administration's credo. Avoid consistency in treatment of the inmate. Manifest caprice in rulings on inmate's requests and needs. Show disdain and hostility, frequently refuse to acknowledge or respond to inmate's queries. Above all, do not base responses, judgments and pronouncements on logic. "Logic" will undo our authority:

Such is the calling of the government in its relationship to the rules and orders that govern the inmate's life. The government rules by fiat, not law, not logic. "It is right because the government does it." It is not that the government does it because it is right!

There's a plethora of official requests each day made by the inmates. An official form, called a "cop-out" sheet, is provided, so that the inmate can directly correspond with the Camp Administrator pertinent to his needs. Requests for medicines, medical attention, books, further forms, copies of rules and regulations, requests for furloughs, additional phone and visiting clearance, clarification of release date, half-way house assignment, matters pertaining to law, inmate files, records, religion, attire, the list goes on and on. All are sincerely delivered to the Camp Administration and responses are awaited with devout patience and anxiety.

When responses do occur, the inmates compare and contrast. Many have submitted the same or similar inquiries. The contradictions and inconsistencies are overwhelming for the inmates. The basis for government decisions on their questions and needs is not explicated. There is no consistency. The results appear capricious and insulting. The inmates lose faith with the system. No justice in prison camp is the verdict of the prisoner.

VISITING

One of the saddest spectacles of camp life is watching inmates prepare for visiting. Visiting is allowed on weekends: the mornings and early afternoons. All visitors must be approved by the administration in advance. Family members and friends are permitted. Forms have to be filled out. It takes up to a few weeks to "clear" them. By phone call or letter, inmates learn when they are to be visited.

Visiting facilities consist of a relatively large room, somewhat sterile in affect; food and drink dispensing machines. The visitors have to bring multiple quarters. All in an outdoor area, fenced in, somewhat esthetic; roses and other flowers on a grassy area under eucalyptus trees; metallic chairs and tables, and children running about.

I sit in the law library which overlooks where the prisoners wait to be called to visiting over a loud speaker. There's always about a dozen of them standing, stretching their necks, peering toward the parking lot and entranceway to the visiting room. Inmates during visiting must wear the standard issued green prison uniform. They are allowed to wear commissary purchased tennis shoes.

The inmates all want to look their best, recently showered, clean-shaven, some with pressed uniforms. No hats allowed. All, seemingly wearing new white tennis shoes. They look like well-scrubbed military cadets. They appear nervous, shy, and anxiety ridden. They will be seeing their wives, children, sweethearts, mothers, fathers, and friends. They are in prison. Some are ashamed of it. To me, they all look like children, ready to be castigated, filled with self-doubt and fears of condemnation, like little tin green soldiers, ready to cry. After visiting, they return proud to have had a visit (most inmates rarely have visitors), happy, relieved. Some have kissed their loved ones;

others get the latest news from home. The inmates feel forgiven and reprieved. They all seem to share their visit conversations with their inmate friends. The entire prison camp has a vicarious contact, in this way, with the doings of the "outside" every weekend.

CORN FOR ALL

Lompoc Camp, a prison, a jail, a penal colony, men condemned by society, the reprobates, criminals in exile, occupies a rare few acres of still pristine beauty: inmates consigned to beauty, nature's irony!

The camp sits on a bluff, a hill, and a mount that overlooks a lush valley. Inmates sit on wooden chair benches behind a screen wired fence and stare out into the valley; across the valley, at the rolling hills but a few miles away, a tree lined river winds its way along the perimeter of the valley. Hawks circle overhead; boundaries of eucalyptus trees scent the winds. All is pastoral, bucolic and serene. The lush area was once a thriving Native American domain. It's near the sea. Hunting, fishing and agriculture sustained previous Indian life. It sustains the esthetic life of the inmates now.

The entire valley, almost as far as the eye can see, is one huge crop of corn presently. The corn feeds the cattle. The cattle supply meat and dairy products to the federal prison system. Giant water sprinklers, standing six to eight feet high, like white poles in the corn field, feed the crop and keep it green and fecund. On a quiet night, it is said that you hear the corn growing. The valley is a sea of green.

On one far side, near the river where the tree and plant growth is thick, herds of deer, like decades ago, still populate the valley. They exit the riverbed hideaway at dusk. First, the does, then the fawns and lastly, out but standing apart, some long-horned bucks. All feast undisturbed on the growing corn.

We like to fantasize that the Indians of the past made a contract with the prison authorities: "You get the land of our ancient tribes. You can grow your corn and feed your cattle so long as you allow the deer to roam freely without harm and to fill themselves to their limits on your growing corn." It's a fiction but that's what we, the inmates, see from our chairs in the low sky: bucks butting heads, mother and baby deer eating contently. There is corn for all in our prison camp.

CAMP RULES AND PUNISHMENT

At a prison camp, for an inmate, there are rules and regulations, crimes and offenses, sanctions and punishments. They range from the serious to the technical, from prosecutions to suspension of privileges.

For instance, rapes, assaults, theft, possession of drugs, telephones, weapons, escapes are areas where all actions that will result in further court charges. The inmate charged will go to the "hole," isolation in the real prison, next door forthwith.

Things, like failing to appear for scheduled counts, failure to appear for work assignments, talking back to a guard, not obeying a guard, possession of obscene photos (their definition, i.e. naked woman or parts thereof), being "out of bounds" of the camp, smoking cigarettes, all usually result in two or three weeks confinement in the "hole," and then a return to camp.

The lesser infractions such as possession of unauthorized books, food, failure to make your bed properly, sleeping under the covers during the day, gambling, loud cursing, fondling your wife or girl-friend at visiting and a few others, result in suspension of commissary privileges or visiting privileges or phone privileges for a number of months.

The least of violations, like wearing a hat in the dining area, having your shirt-tails out, having your bunk area messy, wearing tennis shoes rather than work shoes result in reprimand and/or confiscation of the offending object.

So, one discovers that there is more regulation and sanction inside a prison than outside. There is little or no "due process." The sanction immediately follows the alleged offense.

CACOPHONY IN THE DORM

There are few instances in human life that three hundred and fifty men sleep, eat, talk, bathe and live together on a daily basis. That's the situation in a prison camp. The analogy that comes to mind is the military. Army living conditions are probably pretty close, but servicemen are free to come and go, get furloughs, see women socially on the outside and are not always restricted to a few small areas in a camp environment.

Thus, when in two relatively small sleeping dorms, three hundred and fifty men are squeezed together in two level bunks with all their worldly possessions in a metal cabinet; it's a fairly unique experience.

The first impression is of the senses. One is overwhelmed by voice and odors. Washers and dryers provide a background noise rhythm. The air circulators turn on and off so the sound of rasping wind is constant. Day and night, the inmates congregate in small clusters, talking, laughing and shrieking. To sleep at night before the lights go off at 10:30 p.m. is near impossible. Snoring from every direction is the bugle call of slumber. It is a strange cacophony. Foot odors, body odors, odors of soap, after shaving lotion and musty clothes inundate the nostrils. English language, Spanish language, and Asian languages, even Iranian tongues mix in strange swirling sounds.

Next to be noticed are the inmates themselves. Every race and ethnicity is represented. Every body type is to be seen: six-foot-five muscular Blacks, four-foot-ten small Asians or Hispanics, giant Northern Europeans. Tattoos are everywhere: some blue and faded, others multicolored, on legs, torsos, necks and arms. Half-clad men of all ages walk about, to the showers, to the athletic fields; girlie pictures on most inmates locker walls. The dorms are a masculine crucible of virile images.

117

And the faces of the men, something rarely to be observed in normal society: shaved heads, long hair; black, brown, red hair; beards, mustaches, shaven, unshaven; big flat brows, thick linear skulls, large noses, round noses; pink, white, brown, yellow skin; the weight lifters overly pumped bodies; the computer nerds – skinny, no muscle development; the tall, the short, the loud, the quiet; the whole human race melted together in a prison sleeping dorm. It's fascinating just to watch and listen.

SWALLOWS IN THE CAMP

Barn swallows or starlings, no one seems to know which, are seemingly ecstatic co-occupants of the prison farm. Their straw and mud nests line the perimeter of the dorm roof in plenitude. Dozens of little igloos house the babies and the parents of these birds.

The birds are small with black heads, brownish bodies. They fly, frenzified like bats, doing zigzag circles, up and down, in a chaotic pattern. It's a wonder they don't collide with one another. They are like bees swarming.

In the early morning at dawn, they circle helter-skelter hundreds of feet up, sometimes landing on the eucalyptus trees. There is a high-poled light, like a nighttime baseball diamond light near the dorm where their nests are located. The light draws flying insects. At dawn and dusk the birds, much like bats, appear to feed on the insects. During the afternoon, the birds fly low, still erratic in their flight patterns. They go in and out of the nests. Perhaps they are feeding their babies.

These swallows or starlings are an obvious part of the milieu of the camp. Their numbers increase regularly. They swarm above our heads. Because they always appear to be in a frenzy, they are psychologically unsettling, no gliding, no grace, no peace instilled in us from them. Just their chaos added to our mental chaos. I really wish they would settle elsewhere.

I would rather create a precedent than find one.

Federal Maxim

THREE UNIQUE INMATES

A young drug dealer was indicted, convicted and sent to prison. He is placed in the prison camp. He leads the routine prisoner's life. He sleeps in the dorm, eats in the dining hall, buys extras in the commissary and has a job assignment. His distinction, however, is that he is blind. He walks about with a white cane by himself and guided on occasion by other inmates. He dresses, he showers; he does everything probably other than watching TV. It's not easy to be blind in a camp environment, too many zigzag paths, too many obstacles, too many people. Couldn't they have allowed him home detention?

An old Ecuadorian, bronze-colored, long black and grey hair, worn like Indians, a large face, full of meaning and experience, speaking only a little English, picks up garbage debris with a broom and shovel. He is omnipresent on camp. He has a magic twinkle in his eyes. He's right out of Castaneda's "Don Juan" books.

A Hispanic, about forty years old, when he was 21, dealt some cocaine. He received a 28-year sentence. He has done 19 years in federal prison, in all levels of security. He has seen it all. While in prison, he has obtained his B.A. and Master's Degrees. He was close to a Ph.D. but the prison authorities blocked it. He writes; he has published three highly successful books. All are an expose of prison cruelty and hardship. One book is used for teaching in several colleges.

California Civil Code Section 3520.

No one should suffer by the act of another.

Enacted 1872.

THE GREAT MATTRESS FIASCO

Prison camp issued mattresses for our bunk beds are Spartan sized: about six feet long and three and a half feet wide and four inches high. They are hard, probably stuffed with synthetic cotton like filling. They do not soften to accommodate body pressure. It's like sleeping on the floor so it is said.

But at some indefinite period in the past, the prison issued "normal" mattresses, box like, much larger, eight inches high, seemingly with springs inside, certainly with "bounce" and softness. They did depress to fit the body's size and pressure. Only a handful of inmates had them by the time I arrived at camp.

Recently, by top administrator's fiat, without notice, the old and comfortable mattresses were seized, confiscated and withheld from the scattering of inmates that still were in possession of the few remaining.

There was a hue and cry from those dispossessed. Protest, outrage, a wave of rumor and invective swamped the camp. There was no advance notice of the administration's intent to confiscate. There was therefore no due process. The seizure was arbitrary and punitive. No prison objective was accomplished. The mattresses had been legally issued. Ex post facto was the charge. The camp in its entirety raised its mute voices in objection.

The dispossessed appealed formerly to the higher camp authorities. The action taken by the Administrator was approved, however. The next level of appeal would take about ninety days. The sanction for having the comfortable mattresses was confiscation and cessation of commissary privileges for ninety days. It was obvious that no justice could ensure. The time necessary for the appeal would moot the consequence of victory, if victory in the appellate process were obtained.

The inequity of the administration was known to all inmates. All disdained the action. It was one more example of random cruelty without logic perpetrated on the prisoners.

Inmates here are quick to join voices in protest of the small issues; the petty grievances are well documented. A bad meal, being wakened at night for a random head count, working in the rain, not enough tools for a job; being castigated by a guard falsely. But on the big issues, punishment versus rehabilitation, penal retribution versus education, long incarceration versus parole; on those issues, the inmates observe universal silence.

I AM A RIVER

My prison camp work assignment is "groundskeeper." There are about five to ten inmates on the team. We keep the grass, flowers and gardens around the hub of the camp in good order. We water, cut lawns, add plants, trim vegetation, trim lawns, repair the railed fences around the gardens and lawns, and in general keep things fresh, green and viable.

My specific responsibility is to water a limited share of the lawns and flowers: principally in the front areas of the dorms, administration buildings, and chapel dining room and visiting area. I am the waterman. I boastfully call myself the "rainmaker" or the "river." I set sprinklers, turn on and off permanent sprinkler systems and water by long hoses or by hand. At least one half of my area of responsibility has to be watered by hand, having no set sprinklers and not enough movable ones.

Thus, far the majority of the time, I stand in green uniform, white baseball cap, holding extended a maroon-colored hose. I shoot streams of water on the grass; I sprinkle it on other occasions, by waving the hose gently back and forth; I use my right and left hands. By end of day, my feet, shoes and socks are wet.

The sun in the spring and summer-seasons beats down hotly on me. I sweat under my clothes. I wear sunscreen block. I still sizzle in the heat. I stand very tall, like on stilts, sometimes. Other times I curl over in the direction of the flow. I daydream through the spray. I inwardly smile at my reveries. I watch the giant eucalyptus trees, which surround the area.

I must appear as a solitary figure, way out on a lawn, connected to the buildings by a long conduit, like a diver with an oxygen tank connected to a hose. I like to symbolize that I provide the life force, that what I touch turns green and new and clean and pure. I romanticize my prison work. It makes things easier to accept: to give life when life is taken.

Maybe in actuality, the lawns are really deserts, the flowers – a mirage, and the trees – a hallucination, that I am really dead, that this is afterlife; that I will water now forever, that the flow of life is eternal.

If I am incarcerated, if one human is incarcerated, everything is incarcerated! – the loved ones, the friends, the trees, the birds, the flowers, and the grasses: everything joins in prison confinement. The lonely waterer figure is the centerpiece of his captured, contained and suppressed microcosm.

SATURDAY IS FREE

Saturday, the first "free" day of the "free" weekend! "Free" means that, but for few, the inmates are exempted from their job assignments and not required to wear the camp green uniform. Sweat outfits are provided all inmates for weekend and after 3 p.m. weekday use. The inmate is free to sleep all day, play baseball, soccer, basketball all day, watch TV, read, write, "hang out" with inmate friends, in essence, to relax.

Breakfast starts at 7 a.m., an hour later than the usual 6 a.m. call. The lights at the sleeping dorm go out at 11 p.m. instead of 10 or 10:30 p.m. Inmates skip dining hall and eat their own prepared food. Many soft drinks and candy bars, purchased at the commissary are devoured. The approximate twelve phone booths, for approved list of telephone contacts, are perennially occupied. The camp is buzzing; the day and evening seem longer than on weekends. For most, a Saturday night movie, a CD is played on selected TV screens. "R" rated are expurgated, only for sex, not violence.

I schedule my day Friday night. I have an itinerary. I write my letters Saturday morning in the law library. Mornings, my mind is the clearest. I write to my children, to Vicki, my wife, to the office and return letters to all whom have written to me during the week. I usually handwrite about six to eight letters every Saturday. I re-read all the letters received, before responding. I then discard them.

After letter writing and usually after brunch at 10:30 to 11:30 a.m., I read legal matters, appellants' briefs, writs and administrative appeals. The inmates give such material to me for my comments. I read it and later, Saturday evening, when it is cooler outside, I sit on a bench with the inmates. The benches are wooden, located on the lawns and in the gardens that surround the hub, buildings of the camp. We have some privacy and talk about the legal issues for no less than an hour for each.

In the early afternoon, I outline the part of the chapter of the book I am writing. I prepare a detailed outline for Sunday. On Sundays, morning and early afternoon, I write for about three hours every Sunday. Also early Saturday afternoon, after the outline, I read. I have read book after book, mostly long novels by well-established authors of the nineteenth century; Tolstoy, Henry James, Dostoyevsky, Victor Hugo, et al.

After dinner at 4:30 to 5:30 p.m. on Saturday, I read further and include last week's newspapers; Wall Street Journal and New York Times. I go to bed about 10 p.m. I do not do outdoor physical things on Saturday. I get too much of it on weekdays! Saturdays fly past me quickly at camp.

THE "FOOD FREAKS"

Private enterprise is alive and well at Lompoc Prison Camp. The washer and the dryers grind out their meter and rhyme all night long. It's a commercial venture. Books of U.S. postage stamps are the medium of exchange. An inmate can get his clothes pressed, extra pillows, sweatshirts, socks, anything issued or derived from the commissary, for books of stamps, contraband cigarettes, or old fashioned barter. But the largest underground market is food.

From the farm butchers come midnight steaks and beef jerky. From the kitchen inmate personnel come oranges, cookies, fried chicken, cake and ice cream. Cantaloupes and strawberries that never reach the chow line are sold and bartered clandestinely in the dormitories. Most inmates have a stash of or "connection" to the illicit purloined contraband food. The secrecy of the obtainment makes the items taste better.

At the more gourmet level, inmate de facto chefs cook up contraband meals. The commissary supplies ketchup, hot sauce and peppers. There is a microwave oven in each dormitory. Leftovers from the kitchen, rice, hamburger and vegetables are mixed with the spices, heated and put into plastic refrigeration containers. They are delivered hot and spicy to customers at their bunk side. Some inmates rarely eat at the dining hall. They prefer the "home made" illicit inmate recipes.

While some get thin in prison, there are those who sublimate their carnality by becoming "food freaks." These inmates gain as much as twenty to thirty pounds.

PRISON INDUCES REVOLUTION

It is said that prison induces depravity, that it creates degeneracy, that it breeds recidivism, that it makes for a "revolving door" for prisoners, that they perfect their criminal instincts, and that they conspire to commit further crimes. In short, prison is counterproductive to its objective of abating crime and should either be abolished or gravely reformed, especially at present when the stated philosophy of the penal system is punishment and retribution - not rehabilitation, not education, not psychological counseling, not a plan or strategy for a convict's re-entry into society. It is not that the prisoner is depraved; it is the prison system itself that is the institution of depravity.

The above truths are self-evident but there is a greater result that I see as a consequence of prison life. The inmate becomes political. From thief to tax resister, from murderer to drug dealer, all unify in the face of a common enemy. The common enemy is the government. Expressed or implied, every inmate grows to hate the government. The reasons are variable. The government is corrupt. The government is brutal and sadistic. The government is lazy, arbitrary, and inefficient. The government is unfair. There is no such thing as justice flowing from the government. All prisoners develop a hatred of the guards, of the supervisors, of the prosecutors, of law enforcement, of the politicians. Prison instills into its population the seeds of old fashioned "revolution!"

One is not present unless he understands.
Federal Maxim

WORK CAMPS IN SIBERIA

Years ago in Russia, convicts were sent to work camps in Siberia, few returned! Lompoc Prison Camp is a "work camp," all are returned to society, but much of the camp "work" is very profitable to the prison system. Many experts argue that the only real justification for prison camps is the profit from the "forced" labor of the inmates. Work camp inmates are selected because of non-violence and non-flight risk. They should really be paroled, the argument goes. The only reason they are kept in camps is to add resources to the federal prison system.

Lompoc Camp has basically three enterprises: A cattle industry for both meat and dairy products; an electronic cable factory where soldering and assemblage of all types of cables occurs; a farm industry where basically multiple acres of corn are grown for feed of the cattle. Lompoc supplies meat and milk products to other prisons and cables to the U.S. Government. Everyone agrees that these enterprises are financially very successful.

The issue that presents itself is whether or not a society has the moral right to capitalize from forced inmate labor. The inmates as a general rule despise their exploitation. The inmates are paid, but scantly, from about $20 to $80 per month. They also learn minimal skills at these work sites.

Social perspectives will vary on prison forced labor camps. The conservatives say it is just retribution; the convict must pay back society to redeem himself. The liberal view is that forced labor is unconscionable!

California Civil Code Section 3533.

The law disregards trifles.

Enacted 1872.

THE SAGA OF THE ELECTRIC CART

The mechanical universe is still alive and well at Lompoc Prison Camp. Garbage trucks, pickup trucks, farm tractors, hay balers and old long buses, spew smoke and noise throughout the day. The inmates who are assigned to these vehicles are usually from the car and motorcycle milieu and have pride in and admiration for their status. When they drive through the hub of the camp, you can see their egos bloated. They rank themselves as the consummate camp image of virility.

We, on the grounds crew, however, use rake and broom, hose and sprinkler, sometimes a hoe or shovel. We obviously are the "peons" in the hierarchy of masculine manifestations. So when our crew leader was issued by the camp authorities, in specific, the transportation division, a battery powered mini-cart vehicle on our behalf, we were all elated.

It was brand new, bright yellow in color, a small two-seater with an open back portion for loading our hoses and implements to transport them and a few workers to various spots in the camp. It ran silent. It was non-combustion. It was modern electrical. We had established our image securely in the world of mechanical mentality. We scurried about waving on occasion to the other inmates. Vehicle enthusiasts, in and out of prison, remain puerile toward their motored possessions.

But alas, our ego nourishment proved short-lived. Our team leader was attempting to back the car-cart over a low curb when spotted by the transportation administrator. He stopped his truck, ran over to our driver, and screamed words to the effect "What the hell are you doing? You are destroying it. You can't go over curbs. I give you a new vehicle and is that the way you treat it! Get out, you're finished."

Everyone agrees the transportation officer is a jerk. He thinks somehow he "owns" the cart. But that was the end of the ground crew's redemption. We continue now to carry our implements and trudge about the camp by heavy foot!

A "RAT"

The lowest, most scorned and despised member of a prison inmate environment is the "rat," the informant, and the confidant of the guard. Informing on fellow inmates is the Judas syndrome. It is treason. Informants are universally rejected by their inmate population. They are subjected to insult and assault.

I was recently sitting reading by my bunk one evening in the dormitory barracks. A long white bearded, emaciated inmate asked if he could sit and confide in me. I said sure, I am still a lawyer which status is quasi-religious in prison. He told me that a certain inmate with whom I was talking at breakfast table was a "rat" and to beware.

He said that the person had passed information to the guards about what food products, meat, fruits, vegetables, were being stolen by other inmates from the kitchen and being distributed for consideration, as contraband, to the other inmates. An inmate clandestine food service is abundantly present at camp! Such information put the underground food suppliers at risk. It, if true, was certainly an act of sabotage.

For the "rat" at our camp, there was no presumption of innocence, no trial, no due process. I'll never know if he was really an informant, or if the rumor passed from mouth to mouth was false. Rumors spread like wild fire at prison. But retaliation was certain. Convicted by hearsay, all of the alleged informant's possessions, his blanket and his mattress, were stripped from his bunk area, and thrown outside on the ground in a pile. He is shunned by all prisoners. He is pale, isolated, pointed at and fearful. He has no friends. He is mentally perishing and we will really never know if he, in fact, was truly a "rat."

Our constitution was not written in the sands to be washed away by each wave of new judges blown in by each successive political wind.

Federal Maxim

BLACK CATS, THE PRISON PETS

Do traditional taboos man much in a prison camp? Is superstition alive there? Not really. But it's not because the inmates lack the temperament; it's really born of their ignorance. There are no active superstitions, because inmates from all strata seem to be ignorant of them. Classic mythology, early European religious views, paganism, astrology, and all the aphorisms that have been passed on by such lie unexposed to the collective inmate mentality.

But doesn't everyone know about black cats? No matter what zone of society one hails from, haven't we all heard that of a black cat crosses your path; you are in for a spate of bad luck? Beware black cat's cries my childhood wisdom.

But not at Lompoc Prison Camp, the camp "pets," and there is at least a dozen of them, are black cats: male, female and kittens of the species. They live under the sleeping dorms, they live under the law library, and they live under the multi-denominational religious building. The black cats have no enemies. They parade the camp boldly. They sun themselves openly. The mothers' nurse their litter exposed to all. Inmates feed them, overfeed them from the mess hall. Leftover scraps of meat, chicken, fish are strewn over their domains. The strongest, most muscular of the inmates, play with them, pet them, purr at them. Their numbers grow unabatedly. They "cross" everyone's path. They walk back and forth all day. No one cares. No one enforces a sanction for observation of the superstition. Black cats are safe and loved at Lompoc Prison Camp. Maybe we all feel that we have been "black-catted" already!

MY PRISON CAMP HANDS

Hands can be the most revealing metaphor of a person's existence. Until I reached my 60th year, I had the hands of an El Greco priest: thin, elastic, sinewy, elongated, clean fleshed with an almost religious hue. They were alive on their own like my hands possessed independent brains. At a young age, people marveled at how I could grasp, with one hand on a football or basketball. My fingers were long and strong, like a hawk's claws. They gifted me excellence in athletics.

Later, in the lawyer years, my hands and fingers grasping pen instead of ball transferred thought to paper 100 miles an hour. I could write verbatim testimony of witnesses almost as fast as a shorthand reporter. My thumb and middle finger of my right hand became callused and tough because I wrote incessantly. I filled trial books with my hand held instruments of speed-laced transcriptions. My hands flew along the paper like a piano maestro. I had the hands and fingers of a surgeon attached to the mind of a lawyer.

Today I sit in the library of a Federal Prison Camp and examine my hands. I scrutinize the backs of my hands with horror. No longer delicate instruments, my hands have turned to reptiles. Eight months of watering prison camp grounds have made them shriveled, withered and cracked from the heat of sun burning on them. The intensity of freezing cold makes them brittle. The flesh is water marked, sun burnt, the outer skin mottled and peeling. My hands in prison have become spiders and lizards and snakes. I have bumped and scraped so many plants and limbs: I have picked up much camp debris and hauled buckets and garbage cans; hands are no longer a fine instrument of logic and discourse; my hands now scabbed and scratched and lacerated, are shovel, rake and hoe – the extension of muscle and blood, holding, lifting, pulling and sifting through earth and water and air. They are no longer art; they are function.

The courts must address themselves in some instances to issues of social policy, not because this is particularly desirable, but because often there is no feasible alternative.

Federal Maxim

BREAKFAST

I rise instantly. It's 6 a.m., dress, make my bunk bed army style, neatly, pull blankets, one sheet taut.

I make hot instant coffee, water from the "hot faucet" in the communal shower/bathroom. I don't look in the mirror. My long hair tangled matted, no conditioner. I shave every third day. I know my face is sunburned but I have no pride in my appearance now.

The coffee, weak, stirs my consciousness. I'm buoyant, never depressed. My friend, it's almost a "buddy" system here, joins me. I will water lawns with him later on today. It's my temporary job assignment. We exit the barracks, our sleeping quarters, with coffee in mug in hand. We travel about fifty yards to the "mess" hall for breakfast. It's 6:15 a.m. I'm bathed in warm faint fog as we walk.

The food building is already crowded. We join a long line. We get our trays and one plastic spoon. The spoon is bright yellow. The trays are gray and cheerless.

One big plop of oatmeal is all I want. I refuse the hard boiled eggs. I despise the stacks of white bread. I get a plastic glass. I fill it with fresh cold milk. The milk is from the dairy at the camp farm. It's my life's blood now. I can't wait to sip its chill whiteness.

We join two others at a small rectangular table. We sit on plastic chairs affixed to the table.

It's over friendly. We greet and are greeted. I sip my coffee. The conversation is heart-felt and animated: the food rush is a catalyst for it.

The talk, similar every meal, is a critique of the administrator, sarcasm about the slowness, the indifference, the contradictions in the system, in the administration of the camp. But also there is always the revelation of the backgrounds, the past of the inmates, their wives, their children, and their business before prison. Four at a table, four of entirely different lifestyles coming from different geographical areas in the United States; different in age, in ethics, different education, different crimes, different sentences, the long termers, the short termers; all garrulous now together at the table. We sit on plastic chairs affixed to the table.

We coalesce at the breakfast meal. We unify our spirits. We do the early morning mantra of speech. We hum and cheer each other at the start of day. Breakfast is our church time. We walk out optimistic about life, our life, life in general. The life force pulses through us. Prison has given us brotherhood. It has given us strength, not weakness, not penance.

THE BUREAUCRAT BULLY

Whenever, under stress or pressure, it's nice to have a convenient image of a cruel oppressor to project one's frustration upon: "Poor me, I am not morally culpable. I am the victim of a sadist," and all of the collateral expressions where rationalization of one's plight is psychologically required.

But here at prison camp, there is one camp administrator, universally despised by the inmates, whom I believe really is a sadist, and not merely a conveniently fabricated image of one. He obviously is physically infirm. He is about 58 years old, short, sickly and obese, so much so he can barely walk. His stomach protrudes and hangs its flabby fat way over his belt. He shuffles along like an overweight goose. His face fat shakes and his neck spills over his collar. He looks diseased and dying.

He's hyper-vigilant and hypercritical of everything and everyone. He's technical in enforcing the rules and punitive for perceived faults. He routinely searches inmate's lockers while they are out working, taking personal items, food, books, extra blankets, pillows, photos and pencils. He won't return them. He claims that they are contraband. All folding chairs that are not immediately put in place are confiscated. Recently, he confiscated from a 74-year-old inmate two chairs in one day and when he was given another one by another inmate, it also was taken. Then the 74-year-old inmate used a bucket with a piece of plywood placed on top for a chair. This administrator took the bucket also. Now the 74-year-old man has nothing to sit upon.

Another inmate, waiting for an office meeting to sign papers for his halfway house placement, sat on a wooden fence in front of the Administration Building where the meeting was scheduled. This is forbidden. The Administrator here in question took him into the meeting and asked that his halfway house placement (of 6 months) be cancelled. The other Administrators were shocked at his unjust request.

He won't allow me to get the walls of the buildings or the sidewalks wet when I am watering the lawns. It's very difficult and has no purpose. I set sprinklers, and water of necessity hits the walls and sidewalks.

One inmate who wanted a lower bunk (which, after a while is your right) had to pay him bribes of candy bars and contraband steaks from the meat facility in order to get the lower bunk.

The tales of his petty sadism and petty demands and punitive sanctions are legend here at camp. He's the true bureaucrat bully, not an invented fiction for psychological comfort.

THE CAMP SUPERVISOR

He's really a guard. He's really a prison guard but he carries no gun, no club, nor handcuffs. He carries only keys hanging from his belt. He is large and strong. He is militant. He is the authority here. At "count time" we stand erect by our bunks like soldier prisoners. He marches, chest out, by us, up and down the aisles, counting our bodies. The ritual of the count is ageless: it is the formality of our submission to him, the symbol of our captivity.

But we are not in prison; we are at a camp, a prison camp. Prison to us is not ominous. It is benign; it is a dim reflection of the usual harshness of prison incarceration. It is a satire of a penitentiary.

So our supervisor, our civil servant, our guard is benign: he is an echo of a real prison guard. He knows it. He feels humiliation. But he does not know its humiliating. He talks to us. He explains he has gone to college. His father was in the military. He believes our military is the best in the world. He believes what he does is honorable. He makes good money. He supports his family. He pays his taxes.

He tries too much to convince us – he tries too much to convince himself.

COUNT AND RE-COUNT

Saturday is work-free. Breakfast is at 7 a.m. rather than 6 a.m. We sleep an extra hour. I rise, sleepily stumbling to mess hall. I have milk and cereal, and return to the barracks. I brush my teeth and throw cold water on my face. My hair is tangled. I need a shave. I determine to bathe and shave later in the day. I also will wash my clothes in washers and dryers provided in a ante room of the bathing and toilet area. My hips are still stiff. I will read today. The sun rays are streaming into the barracks through the few narrow windows that exist here.

Suddenly over the blurred P.A. system, it is announced "count time, count time." It is about 8 a.m. "Count" on weekends is always at 10 a.m. Something is amiss. All inmates, all 350 plus of us, must return to our bunks. There is the buzz of conversation. Some inmate has left, has escaped, is the deduction of the inmates. This count is unusual! While we wait, the stories flow about prisoners who have left, have run, have sneaked away, and have left notes in their locker - like "bye bye warden." We smile at the prospect that someone has vanished.

But it is Saturday. Visiting starts usually at 9 a.m. Families have come from afar. Visiting will be delayed. We empathize for them who will have shortened visits because of this abnormal count time.

We line up in front of our bunks. Some inmates still not dressed fully. Some standing and reading: others chest out, attention military style. Two guards, one behind the other by several feet, march briskly in the aisles. Their counting is seen by watching their lips move as they pass. They are counting to themselves. Up and down three aisles they pass, then return to their office at the extreme end of the barracks near the front door.

All inmates stand in place waiting for the P.A. announcement that count has been "cleared." We are impatient. Today is the day we do not have job assignments. It is a free day. We are anxious to do things we have scheduled for ourselves to do: washing clothes, running laps, playing softball, and calling love ones, reading, writing letters, playing chess, and watching the news on TV.

The count is depriving us of precious free time. We are primed to leave the barracks. But over the loud speaker sounds the guard once again: "re-count, re-count."

We snidely smile. Someone really has escaped! The count must be short. Our inconvenience is moderated by the hope that the inmate will not be caught. The re-count reenacts the count.

The same march of the jailers, up and down the aisles – the same counting to themselves, their lips moving as they pass. "Counts" and "recounts" happen frequently. They happen in all prisons, for hundreds of years probably. The same types of thoughts have passed through the prisoners' minds all over all these years: "We hope he makes it; we hope he makes it" has been the silent chant.

After a protracted silence, we are informed that count is over and that we may now exit the barracks. The long line of us rushes out, to visiting, to the law library, to the "irons" exercises area, to the phones. A Saturday at prison camp resumes normalcy.

We never find out why the early count? Why the re-count? Did someone escape? The whole event submerges in lost memory as quickly as it occurred.

FOOD ADDICTION

The kitchen and dining hall lies at the heart of the hub of the prison work camp. It's like a Queen Bee image for the inmates. From 5 a.m. to 5 p.m., food odors emanate from the building. Music, the only music available, pulses and sometimes "rocks" from within. Four times per day long lines of inmates wait outside, then when the doors are opened, line up single file to be served cafeteria style inside.

On hot days, the fans flow dull air and on cold days, the heat frosts the inside of the windows. Inmates hungry from camp labor pile hot food on plastic trays to be eaten on plastic tables connecting to swivel-type plastic chairs – 4 inmates per table – only green uniforms allowed, no hats. It's a "dress up" mealtime. Inmates, like trained cattle, come from near and far on campgrounds to be comforted and fed on governmental food supplies. "Big Brother" becomes surrogate mother of the camp. The dining hall becomes the family kitchen table. Relaxation occurs at the tables and conversations flow.

Where few primary emotions are allowed, where there are no sensualities, where there are no carnalities, where most natural instincts are aborted, eating becomes for most inmates the dominant outlet of libidinal drives. It can become the central feature of a prisoner's life. Food becomes a prison drug. The government becomes the drug connection. The inmate is the addict.

The purity of the food "drug" relates to its sugar content. The inmate becomes conditioned to sweets, canned fruit with sugar water, cake with frosting served almost at every meal; big trays of white and brown sugar to put on cereal, in coffee, in tea, in chocolate, cinnamon rolls covered in frosty topping, jam for bread, all poured into the open mouths of the willing inmate. The inmate becomes the sugar junkie.

When food addicted, when sugar addicted, the prisoner is conditioned like in Orwell's "1984" to respond to law enforcement as the alter-paternal figure – "Big Brother is smiling," "Big Brother is loving," "my protector," "my role model." The penal institution, through use of food rewards, brain washes the inmate into compliance and conformity. At Christmas, for instance, the guards gave all inmates a big bag of candy bars as gifts. The government is the "sugar daddy" – the inmate his "sugar child." As long as the child is obedient to the Daddy, he is gifted with sweets.

There does exist an underground food enterprise. Food taken from the kitchens or the warehouse, or actually grown surreptitiously, is cooked and prepared by inmates and distributed clandestinely to inmates for postage stamps. At least a third of prisoners eat from this alternative food supply. They remain free from the conditioning process, the food addiction, the sugar junkie syndrome: the revolt of the brain wash, by route of contraband food!

THE JAIL HOUSE LAWYER

I spend a large amount of time in the prison camp library. It's called the Law Library, but from the standard law library perspective, it has sparse assets. Supreme Court cases, some federal appellate reports, a few form books, and several antiquated typewriters. No computers, no daily journals, no recent appellate decisions.

But the perennial "Jail House Lawyer" finds refuge there as he searches for the laws that will provide him redress and justice. Jail house lawyers are unique in the strata of all prisoners. They are obsessed, committed idealists. They spend every hour of free time reading law, finding cases, typing quotations, discussing the meaning of the court's words with fellow "jail house lawyers."

They create their appeals, their writs, and their requests for reconsideration with the patience and devotion to detail of Dark Age monks in a monastery. Legal documents such as Replies, Responses, Traverses, Writs of Habeas Corpus, and Petitions for Certiorari are incessantly pounded out of the ancient typewriters and flood to the courts of appropriate jurisdiction. Their labors are labors of love and the last gasps of hopes for freedom, for reversals of convictions, for shortening sentences, for re-sentencing – in short, a desperate attempt to help themselves to the slim prospects of judicial redress.

Much of their legal work is improbable, ill-conceived and doomed to failure. Much appears amateurish, fragmentary, and unprofessional. But some Jail House Lawyers are masters. They have learned the subtle language of legalese; their citations are accurate, their points and authorities apt and relevant. They write writs and appeals for other inmates; they often spark interest in the appellate courts and sometimes prevail.

Therefore, there is both the sham and frivolous prison writ writer and the learned and profound writ writer. They sit side by side in the law library year after year, typing out their pleadings.

I talked with them all. I respect them all. They fill a vacuum in prison legal space. They are the last link for the inmate to the courts. I met one who had a 15 year sentence; he had filed a dozen writs; he had petitioned the Supreme Court at least three times; he had filed in every possible jurisdiction. His last consummate brief was rejected; it was long, detailed, citing hundreds of cases. It was his last attempt. He cited cases and phrases to me, by memory, of their contents. He handed it to me. He said "I want you to have this; it is my life's work." The albatross is on my shoulder now.

MISDEMEANANT

Aren't you TONY SERRA, the lawyer? "Yes, indeed" I respond. The same question in different words is asked over and over of me at Lompoc Prison Camp. "What are you doing in here?" goes the refrain. I tell them "I'm only a misdemeanant. I got ten months. This is my third conviction. I am a TAX resistor. It's not a moral turpitude offense. It's willful failure to pay TAXES, not TAX evasion – for cheating which is a felony. I will have my law license when I get out; I even have a murder trial scheduled shortly after my release date."

"But why don't you pay taxes?" they ask. "Why didn't the IRS just seize some of your property?" They look at me QUIZZICALLY.

I try to tell them I am an aberration. I have odd old fashion beliefs. I am an old MARXIST. That I don't believe in owning anything; that I have no property, no money in the bank, no stocks or bonds – NO ASSETS – that I don't believe in TAXES - that taxes are the plunder of victory paid by the defeated, that only the working class pays TAXES. That corporations pass tax on to the consumer. That capitalism preys on the poor: that TAX resistance is my little principle; that I have been convicted three times, because I am loyal to my principle.

But most all of the inmates in here are convicted of a crime where they sought financial gain. They do not understand my "principle."

NO EXEMPTION FOR AGE

In prison mentality Judas exists in many roles. There's the informant that gets one arrested. There's the co-defendant who turns "governmental" witness and gets one convicted. There's the convicted inmate who debriefs after arriving in prison and names criminal suspects in exchange for a reduced sentence, and lastly, there is the jailhouse "rat" or here at Lompoc Camp, the camp snitches who inform on the criminal behavior of fellow inmates, or the breaking of the rules of the camp by fellow inmates.

.All of these types receive universal condemnation by the prison population. All are ostracized and punished, stabbed, sliced, assaulted; clothes and bedding thrown out of the barracks, beds urinated upon. The outing of a snitch by shouting "Rat-Rat" wherever he appears is the punishment. No one likes a collaborator. That's why there is a death penalty for wartime treason.

Just last week at Lompoc Prison Camp, a 72-year-old inmate on the night before he was to be released was beaten at about 3 a.m. while he was fast asleep in his lower bunk. The assailant got away. He was left with a bruised face, swollen eye, cut cheek and a bloody face. He washed up, said not a word to the authorities about the beating and was discharged the next day.

In prison, rumors are stronger than truth. The rumor was that he was beaten because he had, by a "cop out" (a grievance form submitted to the prison staff), said that some inmates where he worked had put a lock on the storage cabinet containing inmate contraband food, or locked a refrigerator that contained it. Because he himself could not therefore use it any longer, he complained about the lock to the authorities in a written statement to them.

Does this kind of informing sound innocuous, p erhaps worthy of a verbal confrontation? Certainly not appropriate for an assault

157

punishment. Well not so. An old man beaten in the dark while he slept was the collective judgment of the inmates who had locked the container. Any kind of snitching in prison is reviled.

PRISONER'S CONFORMITY BY APPEARANCE

Federal prisoners in camp or on mainlines have for the most part challenged the norms of society; they have consciously engaged in behavior that places them apart from the average citizen; to a large degree they have acted individualistic and in a non-conforming manner. Therefore, one would expect from such individual, creative and certainly self-determined styles and modes of appearance in prison. You would think prisoners would seek to distinguish themselves, like on the outside, by deviating from conformity.

But alas, the reverse appears true. No matter how strong or self-willed or aberrant an inmate was on the outside, here the vast majority seem to morph into look-alike clones, by their own choice.

The normative "prison look" is adopted by most: age, race, social stratum notwithstanding. A prisoner shaves his head, tattoos his body, builds his muscular frame by weight lifting, wears a green uniform with a white cap or sailor's woolen cap. His uniform is pressed; after work hours or on weekends, he wears clean white tennis shoes, short sweat pants over long sweat pants with a sweat shirt, sometimes cuts the woolen hats top off and pulls the remainder down around his neck to act as a scarf.

His beard is stubble. He stands while talking with his hands inside his belt; he greets everyone with "what's going on" and knuckle fist to knuckle fist bump greeting. He raps on the table when leaving after eating.

The prisoner seems to want to identify by appearance as a prisoner. It's a form of inmate bonding and cohesion. "They treat us as robots – we will look like robots." "We are walking stereotypes of inmate population." This is sadly part of the institutionalization of the prison mind-set.

I decided years ago, probably after my first case in this area, that I would not represent cases involving rape or child molestation. I had developed cross-examination skill that was a viciously sharp semantic instrument. I could inflict pain. I could inflict lasting traumatic injury to the minds of the vulnerable when I examined in a passionate, hostile and aggressive style. I recall I did a rape case. I cross-examined the rape victim at a preliminary hearing. She was young and it was obviously a great psycho-drama for her to present her memories of what she considered a terrible event. I examined her. I opened holes in her presentation. I showed inconsistencies. I sneered. I savaged her and she cried and she cried and I still can remember that. The way she looked at me with innocent bird- like eyes as I approached with my semantic sword still visits upon me in my weak moments. Those kinds of things give rise to lots of introspection and moral imperatives. I was a pro bono lawyer in more cases than I could ever handle so at that point and hence- forth, I didn't take cases of rape, child molestation or sexual battery. It was a lesson for me well learned and appreciated early in my career.

SELF-SEGREGATION

What bigotry prevails in a federal prison camp? As you would expect, the same bigotry as prevails in society at large: religion, race and class, but tepid so, and implied but not expressed.

I see Blacks, Caucasians, Hispanics and Asians self-segregate: at the wooden tables, at the dining room tables, at the dorms, around food and talk. It's nothing overt, no words are spoken in the category of racism, but by self-grouping, there is a distance created between ethnics. My generalization here pertains to about half the inmates. The other half mix freely, are openly friendly, work at job assignments, shoulder to shoulder, bond closely. It's a good thing to see from an assimilation perspective.

Only about 10% of the camp inmates are conventionally religious: Christian, Islam and Jewish faiths are observed in the main. A scattered few are Buddhist. Once again as noted above, there is observed a certain degree of clustering by the religious few. I do not see Christian, Jew and Islamic at the same table.

Class grouping is the most prevalent. The professionals, the educated, the rich interlock, network, share their histories, the nature of their convictions. Many will be friends on the outside. The poor and the uneducated seldom mix with the sophisticated. Each economic group has its own diction, idiom, interests and concerns, newspapers and news in general for the elite, sports and TV, movies for the underclass.

There is universal condemnation of homosexuals, rapists and child molesters. Such is proclaimed by the inmates openly and brazenly.

THE SHOWER ROOM

The prison camp dormitory consists of about one hundred, two-tiered bunk beds in a large rectangle room. The front portion of the same building served as offices for the camp guards and administrator. Another space was toilets and showers. The entire arrangement resembled the archetypal army barracks.

My background in high school and college was athletic so I expected open showers, i.e., a wall of showers where naked men would stand relatively close to one another under steaming water from overhead facets. I even imagined army-style unenclosed toilets (latrine style) like depicted in army barracks.

Quite to the contrary! The paranoia of prison sexual abuse and the rabid bias against homosexuality reigns supreme here. Every toilet has an individual stall with a seven foot high door. Metal walls separate each shower location. No one looks; no one sees a naked body. All eyes are downcast in the shower area. Quite absent is the innocence of locker room joviality. Everyone is very serious and concerned about sexual innuendo. A sad tenseness is the ambiance of the cleanup and shower space.

No wet towel fights; no singing in the shower, no colloquies, no joking – nothing – dead silent nothing, but the sound of water falling and teeth brushing.

I recall an incident where victory prevailed on the extra judicial communications from Native Americans, where the defendant was a Native American and the case had political overtones. It was a death penalty case in Northern California where a young Native American was accused of killing a white police officer. He was ultimately found not guilty. The case was attended by Native Americans from all over the country. They brought their elders, they brought their holy people, they brought their children, they served food, they danced, they made speeches and they encircled on occasion the small courthouse in Northern California. They chanted, they sang, they performed drum mantras, all of which penetrated and resonated within the courtroom in which the trial was occurring, sometimes stopping the proceedings. The jurors listened, the sounds permeated, the sentiment of all of us was overwhelmed. It was the Native American way of obtaining justice, not through lawyers, not through legalese, but with fundamental forms of forgotten modes of communication.

THE SWEAT

It's Sunday. We're allowed to sleep in; wear sweats; avoid the work "greens," the normal dress; a day of visits for many, laundry for most. We wash our own clothes, sheets, towels, issued to us, in machines, unpleasantly next to the toilets. Sunday is for chess, cards, writing letters, playing horseshoes, going to Protestant, Catholic or Buddhist service (Islamic is on Fridays). There is no Jewish service.

The Native Americans have created a garden: like space on the bluff overlook, one of the choicest esthetic plots on the camp. Eucalyptus trees sequester it from view of the dormitories nearby. Flowers growing in raised plots between logs glorify the area. Bushes, cut grass, logs for seats and tree "rounds" in circles form a visually sensuous environment; upright limbs of trees carry ribbons and hawk feathers. Circular spirit nets hang from tree limbs, standing erect in the garden. A bold totem raises its heads.

The center piece is a bent limb structure igloo-like shaped half sphere about 30 feet in diameter with the center dug out. The floor is raw earth. This is the frame of the traditional Native American sweat lodge: an altar, a temple, a holy spot for Native Americans, the "womb" of Mother Earth, symbolically.

I rise at 6:30 a.m., a half hour later than usual. I wear camp issued sweat shorts, a dirty tee shirt. I put on my work high shoes, without socks. I know that I'll have to strip to the shorts for the sweat. While dressing I have my trepidations. Will I be able to squat adequately (I have two total hip replacements)? Will I persevere the intense heat of the lodge? Will I humiliate myself? Am I qualified? I look Indian but I am only a "wannabe." My Indian friends tell me that I was an Indian in the last life. I have been asked before but this time, by their invitation, I go but not without serious moral reservation to "the sweat."

It will start; the ceremony will start, at 7 a.m. I get there about 6:45. Five men precede me. There is already a huge oak bonfire blazing. The wood is piled on one side of the garden, presumably from outside of the camp. I don't see them, but later learn that the "rocks" which will be brought into the sweat lodge, are embedded deep in the hot flames.

Someone brings a wheel-barrow piled high with old camp blankets, worn with many cuts and holes but clean. They are green colored. I see that they are being placed over the stick bent skeleton of the lodge. I rise from a log from where I was watching and sitting and help. We throw all the blankets out-stretched over the frame. Then a canvas is stretched over the blankets. Only a small crawl-hole entrance is open. A thick blanket tied to a limb is placed over the hole. The limb with ropes tying it to the door cover is thrown over the top of the lodge, so it cannot slide down. We are ready to enter.

We undress to our shorts; we form a circle around the lodge. We will enter clockwise. It is known that I have hip problems and that this is my first time, so I am allowed to enter third. I move up to that position.

In front of the hole opening of the lodge is an abalone shell filled with odorous burning organic matter, some of which smells like burning sage. I get down on my hands and knees, place my face directly above the burning shell and with my hands fan the smoke to cover my face. I feel blessed. The smoke brings wetness to my eyes. At just this moment I feel drops of rain on my head and back. This is an auspicious sign for me.

I crawl backwards into the dark sphere of the lodge. Once in, I turn and crawl clockwise to a place somewhat close to the opening. I sit with my legs pulled under me third from the entrance. Two had entered before me, one of whom would be the lead spokesman of the assemblage, sort of, in my mind, a "medicine man."

166

The rest crawl in, taking their places one by one to make a circle around the dugout center of the lodge. While the hole opening is not covered, I could see, but dimly. Most of us looked European. I would learn later that all of us had strong nexus to the Native American culture and the majority had Indian blood.

One remained outside; on pitch fork, he pushed through the low hole opening of the lodge searing red hot rocks; twelve of them, in several trips by the outside person, were placed in the center dugout of the lodge - our feet very close to the burning heat of them. The lodge feeling very crowded, fourteen in all in the circle, facing the red glowing rocks. The outsider, the last to enter the hole entrance which is covered by him, by his reaching outside to pull it down over the hole. It is pitch-black now inside, but for the glowing rocks. I sat as if hypnotized by their fiery emanations.

The ceremony begins. Colored ribbons, one by one, are hung from the limbs of the structure inside symbolizing the four directions: east, west, north and south, and symbolizing the sky and earth.

In the darkness each man presents a prayer. Tobacco is passed form hand to hand and as the prayer is offered, a pinch is thrown on the rocks. This is all done by touch and sound; it is too dark to see. The leader, whom I had seen outside, was a very large muscled man, embellished by many tattoos. He eloquently prayed and spoke to us. It is forbidden to repeat any words any of us spoke in the lodge. All spoke with heart-felt sincerity. All prayed for other than themselves.

Water is thrown by the leader on to the red hot rocks from a plastic bucket. The steam rises. A sound like waves hitting a shore emanates from the impact of water on burning rock, creating steam. It is dead black; the steam envelops us. Wave after wave of water crashes on the rocks. The heat is intense. My mind became mystic. Tears rolled from eyes. Every time the water splashed, I am slapped on the face by the rising hot steam.

167

Indian prayer chants started; someone had brought a drum within, drumming accompanies the chants. The prayer chants are song like. The rhythm rises and falls, all sing out together, mouths open, steam being swallowed, and singing with tears running down into open mouths. I join only the chorus at the decline of the song rhythms. I cry out the sounds sometimes softly, sometimes loudly.

Then there is an interval. The hole door is opened. More rocks are brought in. The same procession is followed: prayer, chanting, water on rocks, steam rising. My mind melting: a great unity occurring. I am in a earth womb. I am merging spiritually with the other participants. I am in a state of alternate consciousness. I am elevated, disembodied. By song and thought, my mind connects with the others and in a unity we transcend the ceremony.

Five times we are steamed. Five times the red hot rocks are brought into the lodge. Each time it is hotter and hotter. The fifth time I can barely breathe. The hot steam is smothering. I gasp silently for oxygen. I do not want to faint and I do not.

After the fifth time, a long handled pipe filled with tobacco is brought in. It is passed from person to person. We inhale deeply, blowing smoke, first upwardly, then on our own shoulders, one shoulder at a time. I am throbbing. My heart is pounding. I am a mass of sweat. Thoughts fly from head to sky.

I crawl out. The rain has stopped. For the rest of the day, I remain in a religious, mystical state of mind.

WALKING THE CIRCLE

It's 5 p.m. The prison camp sits on a bluff. Army type barracks, two rectangular buildings, 350 prisoners, dinner over, prisoners at their leisure. It is a late spring evening, misty fog returning after a warm afternoon. Low murmurings of minds released from camp chores. Some playing chess, others baseball, horseshoes – distant soft- ball field with active practice by green clothed men. The weights, the exercise machines, the "iron:" all pressed into use near the volleyball court. The library is full of readers now, the outdoor TV with fervent gazers.

Many sit or stand around, talking, laughing, telling the stories of their cases, the implied stories of their lives. Light wind. Large Eucalyptus and pine trees gently glittering in a lowering sun. Black, Caucasian, Asian men doing the after eating, energy flow, a together-ness. A oneness, a synopsis of good feelings, an image of human harmony on a federal prison camp in a valley by the sea in Central California.

This is the time for my evening walk twice around the camp grounds: approximately one mile, football shaped. I walk with a recently acquired friend. He's 60-ish from Las Vegas, lean, tan, intelligent. We walk slowly. We talk with animation.

First path, we pass over the ridge of the bluff. We look outward, a vista of cultivated hills, early corn crop shooting skyward. Cows are to the left of the cornfield. In the distance, vast flower beds. We walk under the Eucalyptus trees. The scent of the oil permeates our senses. We exchange experiences, ideas, political talk. We laugh. We exaggerate. It is a good moment. We pass the Native American sweat area. It's highly beautiful. Flowers, logs, rocks, wooden chairs, tables, a garden sanctuary form a pantheistic holy spot. Around the first and second turns, the softball field, the young men playing energetically with a devout attitude toward the sport, playing for real, playing like they played during their youth outside – it is a self-revival act of sport ceremony.

We walk back on the other side under the pines, next to a flat grassy field, ground hogs-like squirrels standing upward watch us closely. Back to the camp, our walk ends at the visiting area. Visiting is for the weekends. This is Thursday night. The chairs in the grassy flowering outdoor portion have been removed, the water sprinkler sending circles of spray. A crow caws at us.

Altogether this is peace. It is serenity. It is what all unknowingly seek, a unity of human spirit and nature. This happened in a federal prison camp. It occurs there every evening. Walking the inmate circle is a holy trek.

AFTERWORD

Charles Carbone, Esq.

The prison system - including the threat of incarceration - is the most feared and powerful method of coercion we have. Yet Tony Serra is not afraid. It is not that Tony enjoyed being prosecuted or incarcerated. No one does. Tony was not intimidated because he knew the prison system is crooked. He has seen the abuse of its power pounded out on his clients, and had felt those same abuses quite personally through his time in prison.

But asking Tony Serra to be intimidated is like asking the warrior not to protect his comrades, or the lion to leave the Savanna. Tony is what lives in his heart, a people's lawyer. He goes where the action is. And nowadays, with the largest prison system in the world dismantling the lives of millions of Americans, it is no surprise that Tony found himself locked up where the downtrodden are - in prison, three times.

Most lawyers do not have the faintest idea what awaits their client after a guilty verdict. Most lawyers could not name a single prison where their former client now lives. But Tony Serra is different. He knows that being in prison is a sign of integrity when living in an unjust society. His visit in prison did not result from lying, cheating or stealing from others. He went there for living justly, and for refusing the biggest scam of all. Tony went to prison because he will not give money to a government that has a war on everything.

Once inside the labyrinth of federal prison, Tony did not stop. As chronicled, Tony did what any people's lawyers do: critique and polish legal papers and unravel unjust outcomes. He also sought out the reflective reveries that came once he was inside prison. Tony, however, did not rest with lawyering to the incarcerated or with his meditations.

171

His eyes were on larger injustices. He wanted to stop the very gears that keep the prison system in motion. At its core, prisons replicate the original sin of the United States. Prisons entomb the ancestors of slaves and the oppressed under revamped Jim Crow-like laws that attempt to disguise the barbarism and racism underlying crime and punishment in the U.S. Nowhere is slavery legal in the United States except in prison.

Because the 13th Amendment exempts prisoners from slavery, inmates - including Tony - worked for as little as 19 cents an hour at menial jobs which offer no real skills once released. Meanwhile, the government is required to purchase products from this captive work force before manufacturers in the private sector. The U.S. "free" market depends on prison slave labor, and major profits are derived from maintaining its slave wages. Tony Serra lived this, and his stomach growled.

Upon his release from federal prison, Tony filed Serra v. Lappin suing the federal prison system for the slave wages paid prisoners. He rightly claimed that prison slavery is a crime against international law and a crime that lowers our standing in the community of "free" nations. The case was Tony's Emancipation Proclamation against the involuntary servitude of federal prisoners forced to work for pennies.

Given its broadside against one of the crown jewels of the prison system, Serra v. Lappin didn't survive the first round of judicial review in federal court. It was only until Tony reached the Ninth Circuit Court of Appeals - the supposed bastion of judicial liberalism, one removed from the country's highest court - that the case gained ground. Even in ruling against Tony, the Ninth Circuit was forced to acknowledge that legal slavery is thriving in the nation's prisons despite condemnation by the international community.

The men locked up at Lompoc must have read the Serra v. Lappin decision with glee and relief knowing that Tony would not forget them because he is a friend among brothers. He is in the fight for justice for life. He lives for the cause because he believes that being just is as human as being loved. His fight is the fight of the two million plus men and women who are locked up and thrown away in the largest and most perverse experiment ever conducted in United States history. While the prison experiment has failed us miserably, Tony has not.

Days after getting out of prison, Tony was back in court giving his great orations to juries, spending time making us laugh, dream, and think harder than we ever have, and defending the outcast and the poor. Prison affirmed Tony's humanity rather than weaken it. And, in so doing, Tony Serra reminds us that he has always been free. He has always walked his own just path, and a righteous one at that. Trod on brother, and thank you.

Charles Carbone, Esq.
Prisoner Rights Attorney
San Francisco, California
September 2011

TONY SERRA'S MANIFESTO FOR PRISON REFORM

1. ELIMINATE all prison camp facilities. Send the prisoners home with bracelet monitoring. Camp inmates are nonviolent and no flight risk. Prison camps exist only to furnish involuntary labor for Bureau of Prisons industries.

2. ELIMINATE mandatory minimum sentences and sentencing guidelines: they are excessively cruel and inhumane. Return sentencing discretion to the courts. Reestablish the balance of power in government.

3. MANDATE probation for first-time offenders. Many of the prisoners here are fist-time convicts. Their long sentences make them endless martyrs. Long sentences definitely contribute to recidivism. The option of probation will promote resurrection of lawful lifestyles.

4. RETURN parole to the federal prison system. Parole rewards good behavior, provides motivation for reform, allows prison populations to decline, and tests early, the ability of the convict to rejoin society. There is no pragmatic rationale for eliminating the parole system.

5. ELIMINATE involuntary servitude. This historical remnant should be severed. Slave-labor camps cannot morally be society's answer to punishing criminals. If the prison industry is to continue, pay the inmates minimum wages; the industry will still flourish.

6. RESTORE conjugal furloughs. The cruelest, most dehumanizing aspect of prison life is the forced celibacy installed within it. The sublimations are horrific. The inmate's essential character is twisted and deformed. Let your imagination smolder on the gruesome substitutes created by prison life. There is no psychological recovery from this privation.

7. ELIMINATE informants from our system of justice. They are singularly responsible for more miscarriages of justice than any other component. The "Judas," the "rat," is universally scorned and isolated at prison camp. The inmate sanction imposed ranges from urination on the informant's bed to assault.

8. RESTORE education and job training. Bring back rehabilitation efforts. The puny efforts at education and job skills are laughable. Most prisoners really care about future success. A prisoner who becomes educated and secures a good-paying job is far less likely to re-offend.

9. IMPROVE library facilities. The so-called law library is a sick joke at Lompoc Prison Camp; it consists of a small collection of outdated codes and cases and a few formbooks. The remainder of the library is a random scattering of paperback books and old public library discards. Prisoners do seek to further their mental awareness through reading. Why deny us books?

J. Tony Serra, San Francisco-based criminal defense attorney, wrote the above Manifesto while serving ten months in Lompoc Federal Prison Camp in 2006 for tax evasion, as part of his article, "Letter From Lompoc," published in California Lawyer magazine.